dling the functions necessary to the existence of nearly every organization in the country. Human resources professionals are recognized more and more as integral parts of the management teams in most businesses.

Federal legislation is mandating serious changes in employee and employer relations. Declining productivity in American business is stimulating an interest in better management of human resources. Employees are demanding more fulfilling work and more active roles in determining the future of their organizations. Corporate management is recognizing the importance of employees and the importance of human resources departments. Human resources issues are now issues of world importance. All of these reasons and more signify a new era for human resources—an era when the human resources professional plays a vital role in guiding global issues.

Perhaps you'll be a part of that guiding force.

Ronald C. Pilenzo, SPHR
President
American Society for Personnel Administration

INTRODUCTION

How does $100,000 per year sound to you? Not all human resource managers are making a salary this high, but many top executives in the field are earning that much, and more.

In this challenging profession people may start a career at the bottom rung of the occupational ladder and work up to the top. People who have the education and related experience can enter the field at an appropriate level and progress upward from there.

The career field of human resources management, still often referred to as personnel management, is growing and maturing while at the same time increasing in status and expanding in its areas of responsibility. Thousands of new personnel workers are hired each year. The top human resources manager is positioned at the same level as are other top managers in the organization structure.

The field of human resources management (HRM) deals with all aspects of people at work. Organizations hire people to work and perform those functions that contribute toward reaching the goals of the organization. For this effort, employees are compensated in terms of wages and other benefits. But personnel/ human resources management also involves the dynamics of dealing with and helping the infinite variety of people at work who labor under constantly changing circumstances.

This book provides some insight into the field. You are encouraged to read through it, and consider carefully whether there may be an interesting and rewarding career opportunity for you in human resources management.

DEDICATION

This work is dedicated to Dale Yoder, Ph.D., who has served the field of personnel and industrial relations in many capacities and won many awards. This dedication is intended to recognize Dr. Yoder for the person he is: a courageous professional who has led the way in developing this field. He has given unstintingly of himself to aid the progress and development of others struggling to find their way in a changing and challenging profession. These efforts have endeared him to his colleagues and won him the respect and gratitude of many, many others in this field.

CONTENTS

About the Author iii

Acknowledgments iv

Foreword v

Introduction vii

1. The Field of Human Resources Management 1

Definitions. Importance of the field. History of the field. American Federation of Labor. Congress of Industrial Organizations. Wagner and Taft-Hartley Acts. Growth of unionism. Civil rights. Current status and developments. Future outlook. Career expectations. Attributes of successful personnel workers.

2. The Occupational Field 21

Personnel policy formulation. Assisting supervisors. Relationships between supervisors and employees. The role of human resources management in the organization. Human resources management related to other management fields. Specialty areas. Personnel records.

3. Characteristics of the Occupation **75**

Salaries. Working conditions. Satisfactions. Working levels.

4. Qualifications and Preparation **91**

Qualifications. Requirements for employment. Educational preparation. Professional certification.

5. How to Get Started **101**

Self-evaluation. Kinds of resources. Job or school? Counseling. Applying for work.

6. How to Land the Job **113**

Marketing yourself. The résumé. The technique. Locating the opportunities. The job interview.

7. Getting Ahead **125**

Success on the job. Advancement.

8. The Opportunities **129**

Where the jobs are. Outlook.

9. Current Issues in Human Resources Management **135**

Child care. Parental leave. Minimum wage. Wrongful termination. Risk notification. Health care insurance. AIDS and the work place. Sexual harassment. Comparable worth. New duties for human resources management. Occupational safety and health.

10. Organizations and Information **157**

Additional sources of information.

Bibliography **162**

The field of human resources management is currently enjoying unprecedented prestige, growth, and development. (ASPA photo)

CHAPTER 1

THE FIELD OF HUMAN RESOURCES MANAGEMENT

If you are looking for a new job, it is more than likely that you will soon be heading for an interview in an employment office. Personnel workers there will assist you in locating the kind of job you seek. In all kinds of organizations, it is their job to attract and maintain a competent work force. Personnel workers deal with the nation's most important resource, people, and have established personnel and industrial relations as one of today's most challenging and important career fields.

The work of the personnel office embraces a wide variety of personnel transactions. Each employee must be hired, trained, paid, and provided benefits. The conditions of employment are often described in a written agreement between the employees as a group (a union) and the management of the organization. Personnel policies are generated and maintained by executives and managers.

Individuals at work have problems that are unique to their particular situations. The personnel office helps to solve these matters.

DEFINITIONS

Although there is some inconsistency in the definitions of terms in the human resources management field, those that follow and others used in this book are gaining acceptance.

Human Resources Management

Human Resources Management (HRM) refers to the broad aspects of the field of managing people in work organizations. Personnel are seen as resources, just as money and other things are resources that require management in order for the organization to function effectively.

Industrial Relations

This term is used in a general sense to embrace both personnel administration and the administration of labor relations. It is frequently used to denote the overall personnel work in large industrial organizations.

Personnel Management

The expression *personnel administration* is used interchangeably with personnel management. In a general sense, personnel management deals with those matters that concern the worker as an individual at work. These matters include wages, hours, retirement, health insurance, advancement, and others.

Labor Relations

This term is used in two senses. First, it is used in connection with all workers as a group, or several groups of workers in a plant or in a multiplant organization. Second, it is used in dealing with those matters covered by the work agreement(s) between management and labor organizations in the company.

They relate more to the work itself and conditions of work rather than those things that relate strictly to the individual worker.

IMPORTANCE OF THE FIELD

The field of human resources management is growing in importance. Increasing social awareness in all segments of American society emphasizes the importance of quality in working life and, hence, in all functions of personnel management. The rights of the individual receive more attention as a result of this awareness and of the impact of federal legislation covering civil rights and equal employment opportunity.

People constitute the major investment that organizations make. The direct cost of labor is usually half or more of the cost of most operations. This suggests the importance of getting the most productivity from each employee in order to further the most efficient operation. When a new employee is hired, the employer makes a considerable investment in that person in terms of wages, training, retirement commitments, and unemployment insurance, as well as disability and worker's compensation commitments.

The seriousness of the commitment that a firm makes to each employee as soon as he or she is hired serves to emphasize the importance of the proper performance of all the personnel functions. Loyal employees constitute the backbone of an efficient organization. Effective personnel management contributes to the efficient utilization of the human resources of an organization.

In order to see the occupational field of human resources management in proper current perspective, we should consider some of the factors and forces that bear on the field.

Environmental Factors[1]

The major elements in the current system of working relationships invite immediate attention. One is the working and managing environment, which includes the structure of working organizations; the web of working rules, traditions, customs, or norms; and the economic, social, and political systems in which working organizations exist and operate. Another element is working people—the individuals who manage and supervise and are employed to perform essential jobs.

One point of view emphasizes the process of managing, which is for the most part a people-centered activity. A person whose occupation involves the provision of leadership in working groups is a manager. Managers accomplish their missions through the leadership of others. The essential ingredient in management is the leading and directing of people. The acid test of the manager is his or her ability to provide such leadership in dynamic working organizations and the working relationships in them.

Changing Workers

Newly recruited managers and employees may, in themselves, be different from members of the work force they join. They may bring with them new ideas and expectations. They may be younger, have more formal education, or have different employment experiences. They may have developed ideas, attitudes, and value systems unlike those of more senior members of the work force. They may see their work responsibilities and obligations in a different way. They may expect more or different satisfactions from their work.

Within any working organization, the people who are its managers, supervisors, and employees are continually changing.

---

[1]Yoder, Dale and Paul D. Staudohar. *Personnel Management and Industrial Relations*, 7th ed. Englewood Cliffs, N.J.: Prentice-Hall, 1982, 12-20.

Some of them get new ideas for the company as they gain better understanding. They may change their attitudes toward holidays, overtime, profit sharing, or integration. They may seek and expect more economic security—salaries instead of hourly wages, for example. They may want more freedom in planning and organizing their work or more opportunity to suggest changes.

Major Trends[2]

Both environmental and individual changes are influential in current employment relationships. Both create new problems for managers. Among the most important of these changes are the following:

1. The increased size of working organizations (larger firms, mergers, and consolidations) has tended to increase the complexity of organization and employment communications. It has also increased the separation of owners from the many levels of managers and workers.
2. Industrialization continues around the world. As the industrial system expands, agricultural and handicraft systems recede. Proportions of employers and self-employed decline as the number of employees increases.
3. Work force requirements specify greater and more specialized skills. The working environment thus increasingly becomes an educational environment in which employees may be retrained for several occupational specialties during their working careers.
4. Public intervention continues to expand, with legal and administrative regulations playing an ever larger role in defining work conditions and manager-worker relationships.
5. Managers are developing improved capabilities. More

[2]Yoder and Staudohar. *Personnel Management*, 9-11.

managers have acquired formal training for management, and management education is moving closer to professional standards.

6. The population explosion has necessitated a continuing employment explosion in the United States and throughout the world (see Table 1-1).

Table 1-1. Populations and Labor Forces (in millions)

	United States		*World*	
Year	*Population*[6]	*Labor Force*[5]	*Population*	*Labor Force*
1960	–	–	3,289[1]	774[4]
1965	194	77	–	–
1970	205	86	3,575[2]	1,499[7]
1975	216	95	–	–
1980	228	107	4,258[3]	1,781[7]
1985	239	115	4,865[8]	NA

[1]World Population Growth and Response Population Reference Bureau. Washington, D.C., 1976.
[2]*The World Almanac and Book of Facts.* New York: Newspaper Enterprise Association, 1981: 731.
[3]*Information Please Almanac Atlas and Yearbook.* 36th ed. New York: Simon and Schuster, 1981.
[4]*World Tables.* Baltimore: Johns Hopkins University Press, 1976: 514-16.
[5]Bureau of the Census. *Statistical Abstract of the United States, 1981.* Washington, D.C., 1981: 379.
[6]Bureau of the Census, *Statistical Abstract*, 9.
[7]*Labor Force and World Population Growth* Geneva, Switzerland: International Labor Organization, 1974: 64.
[8]Bureau of the Census. *Statistical Abstract of the United States, 1988.* Washington, D.C., 1988: 522.

7. Levels of formal education continue to rise as less formal programs—literary, radio, television, travel, and others—contribute to a spread of sophistication. Rank-and-file employees become increasingly critical of management error and malpractice as they learn to interpret the data of national income and corporate financial reports.
8. Minorities, encouraged in part by a general increase in sophistication, are becoming more articulate and demanding with respect to employment opportunities.
9. Rank-and-file employees expect and demand more from their employment. As they become more mobile, and as

public and negotiated benefits provide greater security against ill health, old age, and unemployment, managers face persistent demands for economic rewards that usually represent added costs.

10. Enterprising managers in both private and public organizations are experimenting with new organizational structures, new styles of administration, new communications media, and many additional innovations. They have followed clues from the behavioral sciences to new systems of rewards and compensation. They have challenged the traditional view that the reward system is limited to two elements—pay and promotion.

HISTORY OF THE FIELD[3]

Personnel management has been recognized formally as a field of functional specialization and practice for little more than a half century. Its roots are embedded deeply in the past. Personnel management has been necessary as long as there have been groups of people organized to achieve common goals. Individuals responsible for leading and managing organizations were confronted with the need to provide some type of training, motivation, leadership, and remuneration for their personnel, if only on a hit-or-miss basis.

Some of the earliest developments relating to personnel management occurred during the Middle Ages. During that period forerunners of employment relations upon which contemporary personnel relations are based began to emerge. The growth of towns and villages provided a new demand for goods and services as well as employment for those seeking to escape their

---

[3]This section derived from Sherman, Jr., Arthur W., George W. Bohlander, and Herbert J. Chruden. *Managing Human Resources*, 8th ed. Cincinnati: South-Western Publishing Co., 1988, 5-8; and Ling, Cyril Curtis. *The Management of Personnel Relations.* Homewood, Ill.: Richard D. Irwin, Inc., 1965, 21-23.

positions as serfs within the feudal system. Skilled artisans organized into guilds, which established controls and regulations pertaining to their respective trades. These guilds were the forerunners of today's employer associations and helped to provide standards of craftsmanship and the foundation for apprenticeship training that many craft unions still require of individuals seeking to enter a trade.

Until the Industrial Revolution, most goods were manufactured in small shops or in the home by handicraft methods. The Industrial Revolution stimulated the growth of factories as the result of the availability of capital, cheap labor, power-driven equipment, improved production techniques, as well as the growing demand for manufactured goods. The factory system with its specialization of work brought about new problems in the area of human relations through the creation of many unskilled and repetitive jobs in which work tended to be monotonous and unchallenging, and often unhealthy and hazardous, as well. Unlike the crafts worker, who enjoyed some degree of economic security by virtue of having a marketable skill, factory workers lacked security and had little power to improve their situations because they could be replaced easily by other people who could be trained quickly to operate machines.

Originally labor, along with money, machinery, and materials, was regarded by employers as constituting one of the factors necessary for the production of goods and services. Employees were regarded mainly as a commodity to be employed at the lowest wage possible and discarded when their services could no longer be utilized profitably. Since it was the employer who held the position of power, employees usually were forced to accept their conditions of employment on a take-it-or-leave-it basis.

In America, the gradual extension of voting privileges and free education to all citizens helped workers become more effectual politically. Through their ability to muster public support for their cause, workers gradually were able to gain the passage of legislation that offered them some degree of protection. State laws regulating hours of work for women and children were among the earliest forms of labor legislation to be enacted in this country. As time passed, protective legislation was extended to cover hours of work for male labor, working conditions affecting employee health and safety, and compensation payments for injuries suffered through industrial accidents. This legislation, together with the workers' collective bargaining achievements, eventually helped bring about substantial improvements in employment conditions.

It was not until the introduction of mass production methods that full advantage was gained from the developments that had been introduced by the Industrial Revolution. Mass production was made possible through the production and assembly of standardized parts and by the development of the corporate form of enterprise in which ownership was vested among many individual stockholders. Thus, instead of owners taking an active hand in the management of the enterprise, this function was delegated by the stockholders to the new and expanding group of professional managers.

Improved production techniques and labor-saving machinery increased worker productivity; they also led to increases in overhead costs and wage rates. Consequently, more attention had to be devoted to the problem of better utilization of production equipment, facilities, and labor.

By the beginning of the twentieth century, rising labor and overhead costs had forced management to devote more effort to achieving greater production efficiency. They did this through the improvement of work methods and the development of standards by which employee efficiency could be judged. Such efforts led to the scientific management movement, which had a significant impact upon personnel management. The movement helped to stimulate the use of new personnel management tools with which to measure and to motivate employee productivity. However, it also created new human relations problems for managers to resolve.

The development of personnel management into a professional field was aided by the knowledge and research contributions from industrial psychology as it emerged as a field of study. Early works called attention to the contributions that psychology could render in the areas of employment testing, training, and efficiency improvement. Psychological research stimulated by World War I and World War II has helped to bring about further advances in psychological testing, in performance appraisal techniques, and in learning theory. In more recent years, research and training centers have made significant progress in the areas of sensitivity training, group dynamics, personnel assessment, and organizational behavior. Currently in all types of organizations the contributions of industrial and organizational psychology are being utilized to achieve more effective results in the management of personnel.

Within the field of human resources management, the history of labor-management relations is a component part of the broader historical development.

AMERICAN FEDERATION OF LABOR

The American Federation of Labor (AFL) was formed in 1886 through the affiliation of twenty-five craft unions. This federation, seeking to improve employment conditions for its members, became the first association of unions to weather depressions and employer opposition. It was organized as a loosely knit group of autonomous national unions composed mainly of skilled crafts workers.

CONGRESS OF INDUSTRIAL ORGANIZATIONS

The CIO was formed to organize the mass-production industries. Once established, these industrial unions embarked upon vigorous organizing drives. Competition for members led to bitter jurisdictional conflicts between the AFL and the CIO. However, they united in 1955 into a single AFL-CIO organization with a membership of 15.6 million. AFL-CIO membership now stands at 13.1 million.[4]

WAGNER AND TAFT-HARTLEY ACTS

The Wagner Act of 1935 required employers to bargain collectively with their employees and forbade firms from interfering with unionization of their work forces. When a majority of a company's employees decided in favor of unionization, it became compulsory for management to negotiate with them over wages, hours, and conditions of work. One of the purposes of the Taft-Hartley Act of 1947 was to balance the bargaining power between unions and employers.

GROWTH OF UNIONISM

Executive Order 10988, signed by President John F. Kennedy in January 1962, spurred on unionism among public employees. This order outlined the rules for collective bargaining in federal agencies.

Public employment is the fastest-growing segment of the labor force. Between 1940 and 1968, public payrolls doubled from roughly 7 to 15 percent of the labor force. Over one-third of all full-time public employees at the federal, state, and local levels are unionized.

CIVIL RIGHTS

The Civil Rights Act of 1964 provides that no person shall be discriminated against on the grounds of race, color, national ori-

---

[4]*The World Almanac and Book of Facts.* New York: Newspaper Enterprise Association, Inc., 1988, 91.

gin, or sex. Title VII of the act enumerates those specific practices on the part of employers, employment agencies, and labor unions that constitute violations of the act. Employers' Affirmative Action plans attempt to ensure compliance with the provisions of the act and to overcome past discriminatory practices.

CURRENT STATUS AND DEVELOPMENTS

The field of human resources management is currently enjoying unprecedented prestige, growth, and development. The top personnel managers of firms are being moved to the vice presidential level in more and more firms. Federal, state, and local legislation require a greater amount of attention to the process of management related to people at work. Conducting and supervising these processes are the business of the human resources manager of the organizations concerned. The advances of technology are being used in the field to a greater extent than ever before. The computerization of personnel data and the use of data processing are helping the management of firms both in providing information and in quantitative assistance in the decision-making processes.

FUTURE OUTLOOK

Employment Outlook[5]

The number of human resource management specialists and managers will grow through the year 2000. Most growth will occur in the private sector as employers emphasize training and employee relations programs. Rapid growth is expected in man-

---

[5]U.S. Department of Labor, Bureau of Labor Statistics. *Occupational Outlook Handbook, 1988-89*, Bulletin 2300. Washington: Government Printing Office, 1988, 40.

agement and consulting as well as personnel supply firms as businesses contract out personnel functions. Little growth is anticipated in public personnel administration.

Demand for personnel specialists and managers is governed by specific staffing needs. An expanding business will hire additional workers—permanent, temporaries, or consultants—while a business that is cutting back requires fewer personnel workers. The size and duties of the human resources staff are determined by such factors as the firm's organizational philosophy, the labor intensity and skill profile of the industry, technological change, government regulations, work agreements, labor market conditions, and others.

Corporate recognition of the importance of human resource development will spur demand for human resources workers. Much greater investment in job-specific, employer-sponsored training and retraining is anticipated in the years ahead—a response to the increasing complexity of training programs, productivity concerns, the aging of the work force, and technological advances that can suddenly leave large numbers of employees with obsolete skills.

Although the number of jobs in human resources management is projected to increase through the year 2000, most job openings will result from replacement needs. The job market is likely to remain competitive in view of the abundant supply of college graduates and experienced workers with suitable qualifications.

Future Prospective Assignments[6]

Future personnel departments are expected to provide staff services, but their director will be a full-fledged manager in the executive group. Several current developments point to this conclusion. Among the most important are these:

1. The new generation of executives is convinced that the

---

[6]Yoder and Staudohar, *Personnel Management*, 25-27.

first responsibility of management—the responsibility for planning—has to include special attention to human resources. As the speed of technological change accelerates, skill requirements must be predicted far in advance. Lead times for many new skills are long. Selection and training require far-sighted planning.

2. Similarly, organizational planning means planning for people. The pace of organizational change is accelerating. New patterns of organization are emerging, and more radical innovations are widely predicted. A major problem is that of preparing employees for rapid change and reducing their resistance to it.
3. Investments in people are expanding. A firm cannot afford to regard these investments lightly; they must be conserved and protected. Planning and organizing must build on these investments, using modern training and development programs. The executive group must recognize the economics of investments in people, the costs and benefits of training /development programs, and the contributions of new learning theory and related programs.
4. Problems of employee commitment and motivation become increasingly difficult as citizens become more sophisticated, mobile, and economically secure. New reward systems must be developed. Top management cannot assume labor costs as fixed for the future. Executive decisions must take advantage of new work theory and a new package approach to rewards.
5. Increasing employment of professional workers, including scientists and engineers, requires new patterns of day-to-day administration. Top management cannot expect line managers to change without guidance and assistance. Transitional, updating refresher programs must be provided, prescribed, and supported by executive action.
6. Multinational operations also create a new demand for management development. Selecting and preparing man-

agers to work in foreign cultures and having them ready when needed requires informed planning and decisions at the top executive level.

7. For successful competition, an enterprise must innovate and experiment in its management of human resources. Labor costs can be reduced as productivity increases. Alert top managements will authorize and encourage such experiments.
8. Changing public policy on the employment of human resources adds to the complexity of personnel management. Rising minimum wages affect rates at higher levels in wage and salary structures. Rising public benefits create new problems for financial reward systems. Improved public employment services increase labor mobility and the range of available job choices. Campaigns against poverty, dropouts, and discrimination propose that individual firms accept increasing responsibilities.

Educational Implications

Personnel directors and departments are expected to provide the traditional personnel services for management, and the head of the division is being drafted for service in management—top management—at the executive level. Personnel executives must not only be specialists in the many functions they perform, but they now require a broader knowledge of general management in action. This trend has created problems for personnel managers; not all of them are confident about their capabilities in handling the newer, added responsibilities.

Much of the current popular impression of human resources managers and jobs shows little knowledge of these developments. Movie and television characters in the personnel role still act as staff to management. They are concerned with the technical services to management that have been traditional. Personnel managers are characterized as specialists in services rather than as managers first and then specialists in the management of human resources. All managers must have a thorough grounding in the theory, policy, and practice of managing people. At the same time, the personnel manager must qualify as a manager and be prepared to accept line responsibilities and to contribute to the planning and decision making of line executives. The personnel manager must have the capability to move to various management positions in order to be promoted to top management. Those who plan careers with an emphasis on the management of people must make sure they are educationally prepared for careers in management.

CAREER EXPECTATIONS

People entering the field of human resources management have every right to expect a successful and satisfying career in the field. Those qualified, such as people with college degrees, may enter the field at the lower levels of management or the level of first line supervision. Those with lesser qualifications can still enter the field at the clerical or technical level and expect to find satisfying employment.

Since the field is growing, there is every reason to believe that there will be promotion opportunities for those who apply themselves and learn the substance and processes of personnel management. At both the managerial and the white collar level, workers in personnel who apply themselves and learn more about the field will have opportunities for more responsibility and broader application of their knowledge and experience.

Some people will prefer to specialize in particular areas such as wage and salary administration. Others will prefer to remain generalists dealing with all the technical aspects of the field. There are opportunities for advancement for both of these types of personnel workers.

Successful personnel workers respond to the needs and directives of management. (ASPA photo)

ATTRIBUTES OF SUCCESSFUL PERSONNEL WORKERS

Personnel work is office work. The work is performed in pleasant surroundings in comfortable places that are generally clean and free from excessive noise.

Personnel workers deal with paper and data as much as with people. The paperwork entails the completion of forms in order to record or obtain necessary information. This information is collected and held in personnel files in the personnel office. Personnel workers also have to know other job-related information, such as how to credit vacation time to workers and how to figure sick leave credits. Personnel workers also deal with people in that they interview and test applicants for jobs and advise employees of their benefits and rights at work. Personnel data are typically entered, stored, and retrieved using computers.

The success of personnel workers is dependent on their ability to perform the above kinds of tasks. Their attitudes toward the work they do will probably, more than any other factor, determine their success or failure in the job. Personnel workers must be able to carry out their duties on a fairly continuous basis. Both the employees and the management of an organization depend on the workers to carry out their duties, whether they feel well or not, whether it is raining or shining, hot or cold. When a job-offer letter has to go out, it must go out whether it is the seventh or the seventieth letter of the day. Willingness to carry out assigned duties even under adverse circumstances will be necessary to succeed in human resources management.

The attitude of personnel workers must be cooperative and supportive toward fellow workers. Personnel workers labor for all employees of the organization, not just the boss of the personnel office. Successful personnel workers accept the obligation to perform for the benefit of all employees because all employees depend upon the completeness and accuracy of the work of the personnel office.

Successful personnel workers respond to the needs and directives of management. They are cooperative and supportive of management's efforts to utilize human resources to the fullest, while also ensuring the fairest treatment possible for all employees. Management has the responsibility for running the organization and keeping it in business; if a person cannot support management in this effort, he or she should not be in personnel work.

Performing administrative matters related to personnel—record keeping, promotions, and wage and salary classifications—are an important part of work in human resources management. (TAB Products Company photo)

CHAPTER 2

THE OCCUPATIONAL FIELD

PERSONNEL POLICY FORMULATION

The personnel department has tremendous influence over the day-to-day activities of everyone in an organization through its relationship with top managers in their policy formulation procedure. The top management of a company is a small group of its most important executives—usually officers—held responsible by the board of directors for operating the enterprise efficiently. One of top management's primary duties is determining policy, deciding the rules under which the organization will be managed. One of the chief responsibilities of the personnel director is that of advising top management while it is in the process of formulating human resources policy.

Suppose, for example, that management is putting together a new employee vacation policy. We say, "Joe has a two-week vacation each year." But we seldom consider the thought and care that have gone into determining exactly what rules govern the length of Joe's vacation, when he gets it, and other things about it.

Is he eligible for a two-week vacation no matter how recently he came to the company, or must he have been employed for a certain length of time? If he has been on the payroll half that long, is he entitled to a one-week vacation? Will he always be eligible for just two weeks each year, or will he be entitled to more as his length of service with the company increases? Is his vacation to be with or without pay? Instead of taking time off, would Joe be permitted to work as usual during his vacation period? If he is allowed to do this, will he receive both his regular wages and his vacation pay? Can he take his vacation whenever he chooses, or is he assigned a time for it? Is his vacation a "gift" from the company as an expression of appreciation for loyal service, or is it something Joe has "earned"? If it is a gift, is he entitled to vacation pay even if he quits his job the day he leaves for vacation? If it is earned, and if Joe is fired for stealing company property, is he eligible at the time of discharge to receive the portion of vacation pay earned as of that date?

These questions have many implications; several pages could be written about each. And so is it with all of the personnel policies that must be established if the organization is to function smoothly—policies relating to wages, leaves of absence, pensions, transfers from job to job, disciplinary matters, promotions, employee grievances, and many others. It is the responsibility of the personnel director to consult with and advise top management in the formulation of such human resources policies.

ASSISTING SUPERVISORS

Not infrequently a personnel worker is called upon to advise a group leader, or perhaps a major executive, how to improve her or his relationships with subordinates. In one office, a clerk quit his job "because the boss never even says 'hello' in the morning or 'good night' when I leave. I don't mind his criticizing my work when this is justified, but I'm tired of being ignored!" The personnel worker investigated the situation and found that other clerks in the department felt the same way. The personnel worker tipped off the supervisor, who was amazed to discover how quickly employees responded to a cheery "good morning" and to an occasional kind word for a job well done. The atmosphere in the office changed completely, and each day more work got accomplished. The single most valuable contribution a personnel worker can make is that of helping supervision at all levels to cement the boss-employee relationship.

RELATIONSHIPS BETWEEN SUPERVISORS AND EMPLOYEES

It is a truism that a chain is only as strong as its weakest link. In the same way an organization is as strong—as effective—as the individual relationships between its supervisors and the employees reporting directly to them.

How an employee and boss get on together, the extent to which they enjoy mutual respect, and the degree to which each spontaneously backs up the other in time of crisis—these are the keys to determining whether an organization will function smoothly and how effective it will be in attaining its objectives. This is why the relationship between worker and supervisor must be regarded as highly personal and why the most important obligation of the personnel worker is to use every opportunity to help build, maintain, and cement these relationships throughout the organization. Human resources workers must, at all costs, guard against interfering with them.

John was a fine administrative assistant and was recognized throughout the company as one of the best. He was among the few people who could get along harmoniously with his immediate supervisor, an absent-minded, cantankerous curmudgeon who forgot important details unless reminded of them—usually by John. One day, obviously upset, John came to the personnel department: most of the other administrative assistants had received salary increases, but he had not. He was sure he merited one and that his boss merely had neglected to take care of the matter. What could be done? Without a moment's hesitation the personnel worker told him to take the problem to the man for whom he worked. The employee relations worker emphasized that the matter rested solely between John and his boss and that the human resources department had nothing to do with it. He had considered going to his boss, John responded, but could not bring himself to do so. His boss was difficult at best, and now was not a time to approach him on a matter of this kind, for he was deeply absorbed in a demanding engineering problem of vital importance to the company. If facing that boss was his only alternative, he would have to consider seeking a job elsewhere. He left the human resources department disappointed, though understanding why the personnel worker would not intercede in his behalf as he had hoped. The next day the personnel worker happened to see John's boss in the corridor and, without mentioning his visit, said casually that in going over the records she had noticed that it was past time for John to have a salary increase if he merited one. John's boss thanked her for the reminder. A week later John received a raise. He rushed to thank the personnel worker. She chided John, however, saying, "Thank your boss, not me. You work for him, not me. He gave you the raise, not me! Apparently he is deeply engrossed in this project right now and was simply not aware of the oversight. He is certainly appreciative of your merits and is willing to reward you for them."

In another company, at the end of a highly successful year in which exceptionally high profits had been realized, management decided to give all employees a bonus—an unprecedented thing for the corporation to do. The announcement was to be signed by the president and posted on the bulletin board. But the personnel department objected. Though the final announcement made it clear that the bonus came from the company, each employee's copy of the annoucement was signed by an immediate superior.

There are many ways in which the relationship between an employee and an immediate supervisor can be improved, and the personnel worker should take advantage of each opportunity to strengthen the organization.

THE ROLE OF HUMAN RESOURCES MANAGEMENT IN THE ORGANIZATION

The human resources office of any organization performs several functions. One of its primary duties is to keep the organization staffed with the best-qualified personnel available. Another vital function is to perform administrative matters related to personnel—record keeping, promotions, wage and salary classifications, and processing and keeping track of vacation credits and sick leave taken. The personnel office is also responsible for dealing with the human resources aspects of the overall management of the organization.

HUMAN RESOURCES MANAGEMENT RELATED TO OTHER MANAGEMENT FIELDS

Some management functions must be performed in all organizations. Brief descriptions of these functions follow.[7]

Financing

Any organization must be funded. There must be a source of money to establish and operate the organization.

Budgeting and Accounting

The money that is available through financing must be allocated to the various departments and sections of an organiza-

[7] Steade, Richard D. and James R. Lowry. *Business: An Introduction.* 11th ed. Cincinnati: South-Western Publishing Co., 1987.

tion in order for them to operate. This allocation of monies is called a budget: a statement of how funds are to be spent in order to carry out the purpose of the organization. As the money is spent, it must be accounted for. This is what budgeting and accounting are all about.

Human Resources Management

The human resources aspect of management is handled through personnel or human resources management. The functions performed under this category are described in more detail in sections that follow.

Production/Service

Most organizations have as their purpose either the manufacture of a product or the providing of a service. Production involves the acquisition of materials, their processing, and their distribution for sale. Service can include a variety of things, from financial services to repairing a TV set.

Management

Managing includes planning, organizing, directing, and controlling the activities of the organization. All managers must perform these activities in the execution of the particular technical functions they perform in their areas of specialty.

Legislative

All organizations exist and function within a framework of law—federal, state, and local. It is the obligation of management to ensure that the organization pays the proper minimum wage and operates within the requirements of environmental safety and health, equal employment opportunity legislation, and other laws and regulations.

From all this it can be seen that human resources management is one of the central functions performed in the management of all enterprises, private or public, profit or nonprofit, large or small.

SPECIALTY AREAS

In a large enterprise, the human resources department might be divided into two managerial categories—personnel relations and labor relations—and further divided into specialty or functional sections. Seven sections are used in this book to illustrate a possible structure. Typical tasks performed within these sections of the human resources department are shown in the organization chart at the end of this chapter and are briefly described below.

Employment and Placement

This section has principal responsibility for finding and placing employees, including recruitment, interviewing, testing, selection, placement, promotion, transfer, and termination.

There are specialized techniques for recruiting job applicants, and there is an art to selecting those best suited for job openings. The employment interviewer must identify the most qualified candidates, and from them the supervisor makes a final choice. Supervisors must have confidence in the interviewers because they depend on their judgments to find the right person for each job opening.

The size of a company plays a part in determining which member of the personnel department team performs the interviewing function. Usually in a large department it is the duty of one or more specialists while the personnel manager maintains general supervision. In all cases, of course, the manager establishes the basic policies and procedures to be followed. In a smaller company the manager may do some or all of the interviewing. The personnel department serves as a filter, screening job applicants who will ultimately be hired by the supervisor in whose department a vacancy exists.

An interview is not merely a conversation, though a skilled interviewer tries to make it seem so. The interviewer must endeavor to elicit information that reveals the applicant's character, note clues to personality makeup, ascertain what the applicant's schooling and work experience have been, and determine what the applicant's career objectives are. Though much of the latter information can be gleaned from the application form or résumé, if an effective appraisal of the candidate's potential is to be made, the interviewer must be familiar with questioning techniques designed to bring out specific information and reveal the applicant's personal feelings in areas important to the company. For some jobs the candidate's dress, attitude, and general behavior may be important; for others these may be of little importance. The procedure must be performed carefully and within Equal Employment Opportunity (EEO) guidelines, which will be discussed later.

The value of using psychological tests in the course of interviewing is controversial, and psychologists justifiably frown upon their use by persons not trained to administer them properly and to interpret results accurately. Certain tests have been devised specifically for the use of those untrained in psychology, and in some companies employment interviewers are called upon to use them. Test ratings should be used sparingly, however, and never exclusively, to determine whether an applicant is qualified to be hired.

Typical titles for the person who conducts initial employment interviews are *employment manager, employment supervisor*, or *personnel assistant*. This person's principal duties include planning for staffing requirements; recruiting personnel for sales, technical, nonprofessional, professional, supervisory, and managerial positions; analyzing jobs and preparing job descriptions; processing transfers, promotions, terminations, layoffs, returns from layoffs, and claims for severance pay; and conducting exit interviews.

When you apply for a job, you can expect to complete a form. Then you will be interviewed and possibly tested. If you are selected for the job, it is usually because you have received approval from the person who will be your immediate supervisor. The duties you perform in the job will be the result of the supervisor and the employment manager getting together and describing in some detail the kinds of work that must be performed in that position.

Determining Personnel Requirements. Considerable lead time is required to recruit, select, and train employees for many of the jobs in an organization. Therefore, job vacancies must be anticipated as far as possible in advance. A company's work load and personnel requirements are determined by its product, sales, or services provided. Effective planning helps the company anticipate customer demand. The pressure of unions for stabilized employee turnover has caused many companies to devote more time to human resources planning in an effort to minimize fluctuations in the work force.

Through the use of forecasting techniques, a company may be able to discover cyclical trends affecting sales and organizational growth and to project these trends into the future as a means of predicting its own business activity. Temporary fluctuations in the rate of production need not necessitate any changes in the size of the regular work force. Adjustments to temporary increases in the work load can be accomplished through the use of overtime, by subcontracting some of the work, or by utilizing the services of companies that supply temporary personnel.

Public agencies such as educational institutions and hospitals must also operate efficiently within established budgets. Many of these public enterprises experience fluctuations in the demand for their services.

The personnel requirements of an organization, which are determined by the volume of work being performed by it, must be translated into specific job allocations. Authority to fill positions is limited by departmental payroll budgets that specify the positions to be filled and the wages to be paid to each new worker.

Recruiting Personnel. An organization can develop an effective work force only if it is able to recruit the best-qualified people. Such individuals may already be employed in other positions in the organization or they may be recruited from the outside.

An employer should neither neglect nor rely too heavily upon internal sources for personnel. The use of internal sources can be beneficial to morale and can enable an organization to realize a return from the training investment it has in its employees. Computerized information systems have made possible the use of data banks covering the qualifications of each employee. An organization can screen its entire work force quickly to locate candidates who have the qualifications required to fill a specific opening. These data can also be used to prepare personnel reports pertaining to work force statistics, labor costs, absenteeism, and employee turnover by job classes, department, or for the organization as a whole. Computerized data can be used to plan the career paths of people in organizations and to anticipate the openings and staffing requirements that will result from attrition.

There are many sources from which personnel may be recruited. The major external sources of applicants include the following:

Advertising
Educational institutions
Employment agencies
Employee referrals
Unsolicited applications
Professional organizations
Labor unions

The effectiveness of advertising as a recruitment device depends on the nature of the appeal that it makes to readers. The growing demand for people with the advanced education required for jobs in the scientific, technical, or administrative fields has prompted many employers to do more recruiting at educational institutions. These institutions screen out many of the less interested or less capable students. Most schools and colleges operate placement services that provide the personal history records of those graduates who seek employment. These services can be of assistance to recruiters by helping them to locate and to arrange interviews with qualified candidates and to disseminate company brochures, handbooks, and other literature about the company to interested persons.

Employment agencies differ considerably in terms of their policies, services, costs, and the type of applicants that can be obtained through them. Some agencies are publicly supported or are operated on a nonprofit basis, while others operate as profit-making enterprises and charge a fee to the applicant or the employer. Public employment offices are maintained in most of the larger communities throughout the nation, and part-time offices are located in many of the smaller ones. Because they charge fees, private agencies tend to provide more specialized employment services than public agencies, and they often cater to a specific type of clientele. The growing need for people with proven managerial ability and experience has encouraged the growth of consulting firms that specialize in the recruitment of management personnel.

Employees may help their employer locate qualified applicants by referring friends and acquaintances to job openings. High morale can make employees boosters of their organization and can contribute to the recruitment effort.

Most companies receive inquiries about employment from people representing a variety of backgrounds and qualifications. Unsolicited sources may not yield a very high percentage of acceptable candidates, but they should not be ignored. The fact that individuals take the initiative to apply for employment may indicate that they have a definite interest in the company.

Many professional organizations operate a placement service for the benefit of members and employers. The regional and national meetings of technical and professional societies attract many recruiters. Labor unions are a principal source of applicants for blue collar jobs.

Generally underdeveloped sources of workers include the culturally and economically disadvantaged. Because of their lack of education or job skills, or because they had a past record that was considered undesirable, disadvantaged members of society have had little chance of being selected for employment, much less being sought for it. Contemporary programs now seek people for jobs.

Women can be recruited through both conventional and special sources. It should be understood, however, that all recruiting must be performed within the provisions of the following legislation: 1964 Civil Rights Act, Title VII; Executive Orders; Age Discrimination in Employment Acts; Vocational Rehabilitation Act of 1973; Vietnam-Era Veterans Readjustment Act of 1974; Immigration Reform and Control Act of 1986; and state and local employment laws.

Wage and Salary Administration

This section of the personnel department has principal responsibility for coordinating the wage and salary program in an organization.

Although a company need not deal with all of its employees in precisely the same manner, all want to be treated equitably. It would not do, for example, for salaries to be increased every twelve months in one department and only eighteen months in another. Nor would it be fair for one supervisor to increase the hourly pay rate of machinists in a department by five cents while another supervisor in the same shop gives an eight-cent raise to workers doing the same type of work. There are special techniques for avoiding inequities of this kind, and the essence of wage and salary administration is the application of these techniques.

When an employee of a small company receives an increase in her or his compensation, the decision to grant it usually has been made by the employer. But when those on the payroll of a large company are recipients of such an increase, they seldom have any concept of its cost to their employer or the amount of time and deliberation that has gone into determining how large the raise is to be.

The wage and salary administrator must make a detailed study of the company's pay rates compared with those of nearby firms that depend upon the same labor market. This calls for a community wage and salary survey. For this to be accurate, comparison cannot be made on the basis of job titles alone; an accounting clerk in one firm, for example, may be performing far more difficult or much easier tasks than an accounting clerk in another. Instead, a comparison is made between the amount paid in the personnel worker's company for performing a specified combination of tasks—no matter what the job title—with that paid in other companies for (as nearly as possible) the same mixture of duties. The degree of similarity between jobs is determined by matching previously prepared job descriptions item by item.

The result of such a survey is not the only factor upon which the personnel director's recommendations are based. Any increases or decreases in cost of living that may have occurred since the last pay adjustment was made, as well as changes in compensation contemplated by nearby companies and other pertinent factors in the labor market, must also be considered.

The wage and salary administrators must compile the statistics that the personnel director needs to decide policy recommendations. The personnel director will be expected to furnish top management with statistics to help them make the final determination. For example, let us assume that there are 4,000 hourly wage-earners in the company and that they work an average of 40 hours per week. Each must be paid for 2,080 (40×52) hours per year, including vacation time. If each receives a pay increase of one cent per hour, the cost to the company will be $20.80 (2,080 × .01) yearly per person, or $83,200 ($20.80 × 4,000) yearly for all hourly paid employees.

Now let us further suppose that there are 300 clerical workers in the company on the pay scales indicated.

From this demonstration you see that when the personnel director undertakes to prepare annual wage and salary adjustment recommendations, he or she is faced with a sizable task.

150 workers	$5 per hour =	$750 per hour	
50 workers	$6 per hour =	$300	
50 workers	$7 per hour =	$350	
50 workers	$8 per hour =	$400	
Total	=	$1,800 per hour	

$1,800 per hour × 40 hours per week = $72,000 per week
$72,000 per week × 52 weeks per year = $3,744,000 per year
(wages for clerical workers)

In a small organization, it may be feasible to manage wages and salaries informally. However, in order to administer them equitably when there are several thousand employees on the payroll, in order to provide a realistic basis for the hiring of personnel, and in order to get and keep the best personnel possible, the duties involved in each job must be spelled out in writing. This means that each job in a company must be evaluated in relation to what is being paid for identical and differing tasks in the same company as well as in neighboring concerns. In addition, each employee's job performance must periodically be appraised to ensure that it is being maintained at specific standards.

Thus a job evaluation is a technique of judging the worth of similar and different kinds of jobs. It can rank the importance and value of one job as opposed to another within an organization. Or a job evaluation can compare similar jobs within different enterprises. It is important to note that a job evaluation does not measure the worth of the performance of the person doing the job; it simply establishes the range within which the salary or wage paid for the job should be pegged.

Before such an evaluation can be made, however, the job must be broken down into its component parts and a formalized description of it set forth on paper.

The benefits of a written job description are manifold. It clarifies for the employee and the boss precisely what is involved in the job—what is expected of the worker. It serves to inform a job applicant of the duties he or she will be expected to perform if hired. It is a basis for evaluating the performance of an employee on the job. And, as previously pointed out, it is the basis also for evaluating the job itself in terms of the salary or wage range established for it.

Once again, the role of the personnel director in such a job evaluation and job description program depends on the company. In a large concern the personnel director is likely to have someone on the employee relations staff who specializes in wage and salary administration. On the other hand, consultants in this aspect of personnel management may be called in, with the personnel director acting as liaison among consultant, employees, and management.

Typical titles for this individual are wage and salary administrator, salary administrator, or assistant personnel director.

This person coordinates the evaluation of jobs for compensation purposes, assigns labor grades or classifications to jobs, establishes and maintains wage and salary structures, conducts wage and salary surveys, checks compensation policies and practices for compliance with laws and regulations, and maintains records and files dealing with wages and related data.

Do you think you should be paid more for the work you are doing? Maybe you should. But the wage you are paid is based on the classification or job rating of the position you hold.

Importance of Financial Compensation. Money that employees receive for their services is important to them not only for what it buys but also for what it provides in terms of status and recognition within the organization. Money represents a quantifiable measure of worth; therefore, employees are sensitive about the amount of their pay and how it compares with other employees. Wage payments must be equitable both in terms of an employee's performance and in terms of what other employees are receiving for their performance.

Compensation forms a basis for judging whether the money an employee receives is fair in terms of the employee's perceived contributions. According to equity theory, every employee expects that a certain relationship will exist between personal input—what the employee contributes to the job in terms of skill and effort—and personal outcome—what the employee receives from the job in terms of pay and other rewards. If the outcome doesn't match expectations, the employee experiences a feeling of inequity and resentment.

Effective communication is necessary to assure employees that they are being treated equitably in terms of their compensation. An effective communication system facilitates feedback from employees concerning the relative importance that they attach to the various financial and nonfinancial rewards.

Determining Compensation. An effective compensation system contributes to the achievement of the overall objectives of an organization by motivating employees toward this end and by providing adequate controls that keep labor costs and employee productivity commensurate with each other. The most common system by which employees are paid is based on time. Blue collar jobs traditionally have been paid on an hourly or daily basis and are commonly referred to as day work. Workers compensated on this basis are classified as hourly employees or wage earners. Those employees whose compensation is computed on a weekly or monthly basis, on the other hand, are classified as salaried employees. Traditionally, hourly employees are paid only for the time that they work, whereas salaried employees are compensated for performing the work they are hired to do regardless of time.

Day work is the most common system of compensation

because it is easy to understand and administer. It enables both management and employees to compute wage payments readily. In order to provide employees with a financial incentive that may increase their productivity, they may be paid according to the number of units they produce under a system of piecework.

There are many factors that may help to determine the wage rates established for various jobs. Wages for jobs requiring specific qualifications may be affected by the availability and demand for personnel with these qualifications. However, restraints created by such factors as government regulations and union bargaining power will prevent the forces of supply and demand from operating freely. Data obtained from community wage surveys help personnel managers determine how closely their wages conform to the pattern in the community.

Because of continued inflation during the past three decades, wage rates have been adjusted upward periodically in order for employees to maintain purchasing power. These adjustments have been accomplished through formulas that tie wage increases to the Consumer Price Index (C.P.I.), according to an escalator clause in a labor agreement or as the result of collective bargaining. Or they may result also from employer efforts to maintain equity and fairness in compensation.

Other factors affect compensation. A company's ability to pay is influenced by such economic conditions as its competitive position within its industry and the prosperity that exists within its geographic region. If the work force is unionized, wages and other conditions of employment are determined primarily through the process of collective bargaining. Bargaining arguments based upon prevailing wage rates, cost of living, ability to pay, or any other factors may favor either one party or the other. The wage rate that is finally agreed upon is likely to be due more to the comparative economic pressures that the two parties are able to exert upon each other than it is to the logic of their arguments.

Job Evaluation. The relative worth of a job may be determined by comparing the job with others within the organization or by comparing it with a scale. Methods of comparison may be made on the basis of the jobs as a whole or on the basis of the factors comprising the jobs.

The point system is relatively simple to understand and to use. This system permits jobs to be evaluated quantitatively on the basis of the elements that constitute the demands of the job. The skills, efforts, responsibilities, and working conditions that a job usually involves are typical of the more common major factors that make one job more or less important than another. The point system requires the use of a point manual that indicates the number of points allocated to each factor and to each of the degrees into which these factors are divided.

The factor comparison system is a system in which the specifications of the jobs to be evaluated are compared with the specifications of key jobs within the organization that serve as the job evaluation scale. The factors of skill, mental effort, physical effort, responsibility, and working conditions are typical of those comprising the factor comparison scale. Key jobs include those of varying difficulty for which complete and accurate descriptions and specifications have been developed.

The job grade or classification system permits jobs to be classified and grouped according to a series of predetermined wage classes or grades. The system has the advantage of simplicity since the job is evaluated as a whole. The federal civil service job classification system is possibly the best known system of this type. The descriptions for each of the job classes contain the elements for comparison. The number of classes that are required for the system will depend upon the range of duties, responsibilities, skills, and other requirements that exist among the jobs to be evaluated and the degree of finances used to discriminate one class from another.

The simplest and oldest system of job evaluation is the job ranking or order of merit. In this system jobs are arrayed on the basis of their relative worth. One technique that is used to rank jobs consists of having the raters arrange cards containing the specifications for each job in their order of importance. Differences in the rankings made by the raters can then be reconciled into a single rating.

Rate Structure. The evaluated worth of each job in terms of its rank, class, points, or monetary worth must be converted into an appropriate wage rate. The rate of pay that is established for a particular job also must give recognition to such external factors as labor market conditions, prevailing wage rates, living costs, union negotiated rates, and legal minimums.

The relationship between the relative worth of the jobs and the rates they are paid can be represented by means of a wage curve or conversion line. The wage curve normally will indicate the relationship between the evaluated worth of jobs and the wages currently being paid.

It may be preferable to group the jobs into wage classes or grades and to pay all jobs within a particular class the same rate or rate range. The relation between wage classes and rates also may be determined by means of a conversion table.

The final step in the job evaluation process is to determine the proper wage class into which each job should be placed on the basis of its evaluated worth. Job evaluation and classification traditionally are concerned with the job rather than the qualifications of the person performing it.

Government Regulation of Wages. One of the principal laws affecting wages is the Fair Labor Standards Act of 1938. It covers employees who are engaged in the production of goods for interstate and foreign commerce, including those who work in areas closely related to such production. The major provisions of the act cover minimum wage rates, overtime payments, and child labor. The minimum wage prescribed by the law has been raised from the original figure of 25 cents per hour to the present rate of $3.35 per hour. An overtime rate of one-and-a-half times the base rate must be paid for all hours worked in excess of forty during any single week. The act forbids the employment of minors between the ages of sixteen and eighteen in hazardous occupations such as mining, logging, woodworking, meat packing, and certain types of manufacturing.

Training and Development

The duties of this section include principal responsibility for planning, organizing, and directing training activities. Although the broad field of training is now frequently referred to as "Human Resources Development" (HRD), the process and function are usually still called "training."

Many personnel departments administer training programs to help rank-and-file workers improve their job skills and perhaps be upgraded into jobs requiring greater skill. Some companies have programs, entirely independent of those devoted to training, designed to develop executive potential among those in lower echelon supervisory positions. Other companies recruit potential executives from college campuses, and still other companies provide comprehensive training for all new employees regardless of rank.

A company's training program is commonly the responsibility of the personnel director. Since training is a highly specialized area, the personnel director usually has within the department a specialist in this field. However, when certain employees within the organization are to be trained, the personnel director does not select them, since line supervisors are the ones who know the employees' capabilities and how they perform on their current jobs. It is these supervisors who can best evaluate the potential of those who report directly to them.

Typical titles for this position are director of training, manager of human resources department, manager of personnel training and development, and training coordinator. The principal duties of this person are directing and coordinating the training programs that may include the following types of training: on-the-job, apprentice, supervisory, sales, and management. This person consults with other managers concerning training and development needs, prepares manuals and other materials for use in training sessions, and counsels employees concerning training opportunities.

If you worked in the training and development section of the personnel department, what would you do if management decided there was a need for more welders? Set up a training program? How much would a program cost? Who would instruct? You would find that if there was a need to train only a few people, outside schooling might be better than internal instruction.

Employees require continuous development if their potential is to be utilized. Employee development programs usually include a wide variety of activities. The primary purpose of these activities is to encourage the development of employees so they will contribute more effectively to the goals of the organization and will gain a greater sense of satisfaction from their work.[8]

An orientation program should give new employees an understanding of how their jobs contribute to the success of the organization and how the services or products of the organization contribute to society. The personnel department is ordinarily responsible for coordinating orientation activities and for providing information concerning conditions of employment, pay and benefits, and other matters not directly under the supervisor's direction.

In a large organization the personnel department provides managers and supervisors with considerable assistance in conducting training, organizing the classes, selecting and training instructors, procuring equipment and other aids, and working with educational institutions and government agencies. Frequently, in larger organizations, these activities are handled by separate training divisions within the personnel departments. In smaller organizations, however, most of the training is arranged

---

[8] Sherman, Bohlander, and Chruden. *Managing Human Resources*, 193.

by the managers and supervisors of the departments that are concerned.

Managers should be alert to signs indicating that employees require training. If production records show that workers are not achieving production standards, additional training may be required. Similarly, an excessive number of rejects or material waste may be caused by inadequate training. An increase in the number of accidents may be an indication that employees need safety training.

While training represents a positive approach to the improvement of performance, it cannot provide the solution to all such problems. For example, if production has fallen off because workers are disgruntled and resentful over inadequate pay, additional training is not likely to increase production.

Training Methods. Several different methods of training are available. In large organizations most of these methods will be used.

On-the-job training. This kind of training is conducted by the supervisor right on the job as it is being performed. It has the advantage of providing firsthand experience under normal working conditions. It also provides an opportunity for the supervisor to build a good relationship with the new employee.

Vestibule schools. Large business organizations frequently provide what are described as "vestibule schools" as a preliminary to actual shop experience. As far as possible, shop conditions are duplicated, but instruction, not output, is the major objective, with special instructors provided.[9]

Conference training. This is individualized instruction by a supervisor where the training involves primarily the communication of ideas, procedures, and standards. This method allows for considerable variation in the amount of employee participation.

---

[9] Yoder and Staudohar, *Personnel Management*, 278.

Apprenticeship training. In apprenticeship training the young worker entering industry is given thorough instruction and experience, both on and off the job, in the practical and theoretical aspects of a skilled trade. These programs require cooperation between management and labor unions, industry and government, and the company and the school system.

Classroom training. Training in the classroom provides for teaching the maximum number of trainees with a minimum number of instructors. It lends itself particularly well to areas of instruction where information can be imparted by lectures, demonstrations, films, and other audiovisual materials.

Programmed instruction. Organizations are making increasing use of programmed instruction in both employee and executive development. Programmed instruction breaks down subject matter content into highly organized, logical sequences that demand continuous responses on the part of the trainee. After being presented a small segment of information, the trainee is required to answer a question either by writing an answer in a response frame or by pushing a button on a machine. If the response is incorrect, the trainee is given further explanatory information and is instructed to try again. Computer-assisted training programs are now being used extensively.

Simulators. By simulating hazardous conditions, personnel may be given training and experience under safe conditions. Simulator design emphasizes realism in equipment and its operation so that the trainee learns how to perform the tasks in a setting as close to the actual circumstances as possible.

Development of Managers. Management development programs tend to be broader and longer range in nature than those for operative employees. Rather than trying to develop skills to perform specific jobs, management programs are mainly concerned with development in the broader sense, including skills, knowledge, attitudes, abilities, perceptions, and personality traits that are considered essential to the performance of assignments. Management development programs have become well established and accepted in the more progressive organizations as an essential personnel function.

Current emphasis in management development focuses on individual redevelopment and on the needs of all management personnel rather than just those at the lower levels. There is also a trend to place more emphasis upon organization development in order to further individual and team growth. Organization development is concerned with the environment and culture of the organization, with locating and solving organization problems, and with making the changes necessary to achieve growth. Management organization development programs are considered a sub-system closely integrated and interrelated with human resource planning, management assessment, performance appraisal, and human resources accounting systems that comprise the total personnel management system. Management development programs generally provide a variety of activities and experiences for participants.

Coaching. Coaching is the process of assisting people perform their managerial duties and responsibilities more effectively. It permits individuals to profit fully from work experiences as they receive assistance from those who have acquired greater wisdom and experience. Coaching is frequently used in conjunction with a management-by-objectives (MBO) program, which focuses attention on work achievements rather than individual characteristics.

Understudy. Staff assistant jobs can provide development opportunities for those assigned as understudies to senior executives. An understudy has the opportunity to learn much about her or his superior's job and techniques for handling it. The benefits to the understudy depend on the time and interest devoted by the superior.

Rotation. Job rotation is intended to provide a greater variety of work experience for the manager. Rotation usually is among jobs on the same organizational level and for short periods. The value of rotational training depends in large part upon the amount of supervision that trainees receive and upon the seriousness with which they pursue their assignments.

Projects. Projects or task force assignments provide managers the opportunity to become involved in studying current organizational problems or in planning and decision-making activities. These can be both interesting and profitable for the participants.

Staff meetings. Participation in staff meetings offers another means of increasing knowledge and understanding. These meetings enable participants to become more familiar with problems and events that are occurring outside of their immediate area and expose them to the ideas and thinking of other managers.

Organizational training courses. Many large organizations have formal training courses of their own for management personnel. While these courses usually are lectures or conferences, some are conducted on a home study basis. Frequently covered subjects include courses dealing with human relations, supervision, personnel administration, labor relations, general economics, general management, and communications. Case studies are useful for helping executives learn how to obtain and interpret facts, to be conscious of the many variables upon which management decisions are based, and in general to improve their decision-making skills.

In-basket training. This is another way to simulate a problem situation. In this technique the participants are given several documents, each describing some problem or situation, the solution of which requires an immediate decision on the part of the trainee.

Management games. Case situations are brought to life through the development of management games. Participants who play the game must make a continuing series of decisions affecting the enterprise. The simulated effects that each decision has upon each functional area within the enterprise is determined by a computer that has been programmed for the game.

Role-playing. Role-playing consists of assuming the attitudes and behavior of and acting out the roles of the individuals who are involved in a personnel problem—usually those of a supervisor and a subordinate. Role-playing helps participants improve their ability to understand and to cope with the problems of others.

Sensitivity training. One of the executive training methods that has grown rapidly in popularity is sensitivity training. This method is used with small groups whose members work together for a number of days. Sensitivity training once had primarily a psychotherapeutic orientation as far as management development is concerned. Its emphasis more recently has been sociological. Current sensitivity training programs have tended to produce more organization and job-oriented discussion with less probing into personal feeling and behavior than they did in the past.

Professional reading. Many larger organizations maintain extensive business and technical libraries for their personnel. Executives are encouraged to make maximum use of these facilities as a means of improving their knowledge and of keeping abreast of the latest management practices.

Performance Evaluation. Performance evaluation is an integral part of any total personnel development program. Performance evaluation occurs whether or not there is a formal evaluation program in an organization. Employers and supervisors are constantly observing the manner in which subordinates carry out their job assignments. They also form impressions about employees' relative worth to the organization. Most of the larger and many smaller organizations have developed formal programs that are designed to facilitate and to standardize the evaluation of employees.

Merit rating is a term still used in referring to evaluations of employees in jobs that are typically paid on an hourly basis. However, with the extension of performance evaluation programs to personnel in white collar and managerial jobs, such terms as *performance appraisal* and *performance evaluation* have become popular. Although performance evaluation programs may serve many purposes, they are designed primarily to improve job performance.

Employee Benefits and Services

Duties here involve principal responsibility for programs of benefits and employee services, including communications, recreation, counseling, and others.

Typical titles of this position include manager of personnel services, assistant personnel director, or director of employee benefits and services.

The person's principal duties include administering company insurance, disability, pension programs, and a variety of other benefits and services for employees; recording sick leave credits, reviewing requests for vacations and claims for worker's compensation, unemployment insurance or severance pay; and possibly representing the company at hearings related to these claims. Other functions include responsibility for employee communication, including newspapers, handbooks, and the maintenance of bulletin boards; directing recreational or social programs for employees; and, in some instances, directing food service and advisory services for veteran's affairs. This person may counsel employees on work-related personal problems.

If you are assigned to the employee benefits and services section, you will deal with an almost endless variety of personal problems, all of which are vital to the interest of the individual employee concerned. A man approaches you hesitantly and explains that his wife has worked for the company for twelve years. Yesterday she was hospitalized as the result of an off-the-job automobile accident. What should he do? You will have to advise him concerning the rights and benefits of the employee in this situation.

The most important form of income security for employees is that achieved through continuous employment. However, every person employed must at some time leave that employment—through retirement, layoff, discharge, injury resulting in disability, resignation, death, or termination of the job. To guard against the disastrous effects of such eventualities, provisions are made to provide for the security of the employee. In this sense, security is meant to be providing some income for people when their regular source of income is cut off for any of the reasons given above. Other benefits accruing to employees under the heading of benefits and services include those intended to make employment attractive and to provide incentives for high productivity and faithful service.

Unemployment Income. The primary source of income for individuals whose employment has been terminated is that provided by the unemployment insurance portion of the federal Social Security program.

State unemployment compensation. Employees who have been working in employment covered by the Social Security Act and who are laid off may be eligible for unemployment compensation during their unemployment. The period of time the eligibility lasts may vary, according to the state law and the economic conditions of the times, from twenty-six weeks to fifty-two weeks and in some instances longer. Eligible persons must apply to their state employment agency for unemployment compensation, register for available work, and be willing to accept any suitable employment that may be offered to them.

The amount of the compensation that a worker is eligible to receive varies among states. It is determined by the worker's previous wage rate and period of employment. Funds for unemployment compensation are derived from a payroll tax based on the wages paid to each employee up to an established maximum. A separate account record is maintained for each employer, and when the required reserve has been accumulated in this account, the rate of tax is reduced. Because of this sliding tax rate, the employer has an added incentive not to lay off personnel, since the unemployment compensation that these personnel will receive will deplete this reserve account and cause the payroll tax rate to increase again.

Supplemental benefits. Supplementary Unemployment Benefits (SUB) are paid by those firms that have agreed to it as a result of the collective bargaining agreements between the managements and unions. The SUB plan permits an employee who receives a layoff to draw, in addition to state unemployment compensation, weekly benefits from the company that are paid from a special fund created for this purpose. Employer liability under the plan is limited to the amount of money that has been accumulated within the fund from employer contributions based on the number of hours of work performed.

Disability Income. There are several ways in which employees may be compensated during periods when they are unable to work because of illness or injury. Most of those in public employment as well as many in private industry, particularly in white collar jobs, receive a set number of sick leave days each year to cover absence for health reasons. Loss of income during absences resulting from job-incurred injuries can be reimbursed, at least partially, by means of worker's compensation insurance. Laws providing for such compensation have been enacted by each of the fifty states. These laws, however, vary somewhat among states in terms of the exemptions in their coverage and benefit provisions.

Worker's compensation laws may be classified as compulsory or elective. Under a compulsory law, every employer subject to it is required to comply with its provisions for the compensation of work injuries. These acts are compulsory for the employee also. An elective law is one in which the employer has the option of either accepting or rejecting the act. If the employer rejects it, the employer loses the customary common law defenses—assumed risk of the employment, negligence of a fellow servant, and contributory negligence.

Benefits. Worker's compensation laws typically provide that the injured employee will be paid a disability benefit that is usually based on a percentage of wages. Each state also specifies the length of the period of payment and usually indicates a maximum amount that may be paid. In addition to the disability benefits, provision is made for payment of some medical and hospitalization expenses and some costs of rehabilitation, and in all states death benefits are paid to survivors of the employee.

Financing. The worker's compensation benefits prescribed by law in the various states generally are financed by the employers through insurance. A few states require employees to make a small contribution.

Retirement Income.[10] The source of retirement income upon which most workers depend is that provided by the federal Social Security program. In most government as well as certain private employment, however, benefits are provided for employees by means of other private pension plans. Pension plans continue to grow. A recent Bureau of National Affairs study revealed that over 90 percent of the production workers in manufacturing were covered by pension plans.

Pension size. Numerous factors affect the amount of pension employees receive. One of the most important factors is the amount of funds the employer allocates for pensions. The share of this fund that is to comprise a particular individual's pension usually is determined by such factors as years of service, the earning level attained by the employee, and in some instances the amount of that person's Social Security payments. The size of the pension also will be affected by the amount, if any, that the employee contributes to it.

Abuses. In the past, many private pension plans have proven to be illusory because employees covered by them have received benefits much smaller than had been promised or have received no benefits at all. Such conditions led to the passage of the Pension Reform Law, officially entitled the Employee Retirement Income Security Act of 1975 (ERISA). The provisions of this act are discussed later in this book.

Social Security. Social Security is not a pension system but rather an insurance system designed to protect those covered by it against loss of earnings resulting from various causes. In addition to protecting those covered against the loss of earnings due to retirement, Social Security insurance is intended to protect them against losses caused by unemployment and by disability. It also protects their families against loss of income in the event of their death.

---

[10] Sherman, Bohlander, and Chruden. *Managing Human Resources,* 550-559.

Coverage and financing. In order to receive benefits under the Social Security Act, an individual must have been engaged in some form of employment that is covered by the law. Most employment by private enterprise and most types of self-employment including farming, active military service after 1956, and employment in certain nonprofit organizations and government agencies are subject to coverage under the act.

The Social Security program is supported by means of a tax levied against each employee's earnings up to a maximum limit. This amount is matched by the employer. In recent years upward adjustments have been made periodically, both in the tax rate and in the maximum amount of earnings subject to the tax, to cover increases in the benefits provided under the program.

Retirement benefits. To receive retirement benefits, a person must have reached retirement age, must be retired, and must be fully insured. Whether or not an individual is fully insured is determined by the number of quarters in which he or she has received a prescribed amount of earnings. The exact number of quarters that a person must obtain in order to be classed as fully insured will depend upon date of birth or, if one becomes disabled before reaching retirement age, upon the date of disability. Retirement benefits consist of those benefits which one is entitled to receive in one's own behalf, plus additional benefits for eligible dependents.

Disability benefits. The Social Security program provides benefit payments to workers who are too severely disabled to engage in gainful employment. In order to be eligible for such benefits, however, an individual's disability must have existed for at least five months and must be expected to continue for at least twelve months. Those eligible for disability benefits must have worked under Social Security for at least five out of the last ten years before becoming disabled. Benefits are computed on the same basis as retirement benefits and are converted to retirement benefits when the individual reaches the age of sixty-five.

Survivors' benefits. Major features under Social Security are:[11]

- Lump-sum death benefit—$255 maximum
- Monthly benefits for widows/widowers with full benefits starting at age 65 and reduced benefits starting at age 60
  - widows/widowers at any age if caring for dependent children
  - dependent parents 62 years or older
  - unmarried children under 18, or under 19 if a full-time student in elementary or secondary school
- Remarriage after 60 (50 if disabled) will not prevent the payment of benefits
- Reduction in benefit payments for annual earnings in excess of $8,880 if over 65

Health insurance or Medicare. Health insurance is the most recent addition to the Social Security program. This insurance provides for hospital insurance and for medical insurance for persons over sixty-five. Hospital insurance is financed by employer and employee contributions and covers most of the expenses of hospitalization for a given period. Medical insurance coverage requires the payment of a monthly fee by those who elect to be included. This coverage pays a major portion of the doctor's fees for medical services, including office calls, home visits, surgery, and various laboratory services.

Other Benefits. There are many other benefits and services that can be provided by employers that are not directly related to the security aspects of work. The cost of these benefits to employers has been on the rise and currently runs between thirty and forty percent of payroll.

Health services. Most organizations of any size provide some form of health service such as first aid, treatment of minor illness by nurses, and routine services administered or supervised by a physician. The extent of the service varies considerably, but

[11] U.S. Department of Health and Human Services, Social Security Administration, SSA Publication No. 05-10084, January 1988.

they generally handle minor illnesses and injuries and provide preventive measures against such nonoccupational illnesses as polio, colds, and influenza. In many organizations, health services have been expanded to meet the requirements of the federal Occupational Safety and Health Act (OSHA). This will be described in greater detail later in this book. One of the main objectives of company health programs is to educate personnel in the principles and practices of good physical and mental health.

Insurance programs. One of the oldest and most popular employee benefits is the group life insurance program, which provides death benefits to beneficiaries. As a rule, the amount of life insurance coverage for an individual employee depends solely on the salary level; however, in many industries there are plans to provide the same amount of insurance regardless of salary. Group medical, surgical, and dental plans, and prepaid drug programs are also popular services provided by the employer through a master or group policy written by an insurance company, by an association such as Blue Cross or Blue Shield, or through some type of prepaid medical practice such as the Kaiser Foundation Health Plan.

About nine out of ten persons in the United States under sixty-five are covered by private health insurance, chiefly group insurance plans connected with employment. Plans negotiated by unions through collective bargaining with employers account for almost half of the employees covered by health benefit plans in private industry.

Financial services. Credit unions have been established in many organizations to serve the financial needs of employees. The credit union encourages thrift by offering interest or dividends on deposits at a higher rate of interest than that paid by most commercial banks. It also serves as a lending institution from which the employee may borrow money at relatively reasonable rates of interest.

Counseling services. While most organizations expect supervisors to counsel subordinates, it is recognized that there will occasionally be employees with personal problems that require the services of qualified counselors. Many organizations refer such individuals to outside counseling services such as church organizations, family counseling services or marriage counselors, and mental health clinics. Some organizations, however, retain a qualified person, such as a consulting psychologist, a counselor, or another qualified individual to whom employees may be referred.

Legal and accounting services. Some organizations make the services of professional persons on the staff available to employees at no expense. An attorney can contribute immeasurably to employee effectiveness by providing help in drawing up a will, giving advice on contracts, and assisting employees in locating qualified personnel to handle complicated legal cases. Similarly, the talents of an accountant can be made available, at least on a limited basis, to employees who need assistance in completing tax returns.

Recreational services. Many organizations have recreational programs. To be effective, the extent of these programs and the specific types of recreation should be determined largely by the expressed desires of the employees.

Most organizations offer some type of sports program in which personnel may participate voluntarily. Bowling, for example, is popular because a large number of employees may participate on an intramural basis. Many organizations have teams that represent them in athletic contests with other local organizations.

Other services. In addition to the services described above, other services have become popular with employees and serve to meet their needs. These include such services as assistance with purchasing housing, moving and transportation, child care facilities, and food service.

Safety and Health

Personnel in this section direct the accident prevention and safety and health programs.

Typical titles for this position include safety director, safety manager, safety engineer, safety coordinator, safety and health officer.

This individual's principal duties include coordinating the accident prevention program; investigating causes of accidents and recommending corrective measures; making safety and sanitation inspections; advising supervisors on the application of safety rules; and establishing safety rules, regulations, and standards. This person also conducts safety education programs, prepares safety manuals, works closely with the medical services department in providing emergency treatment for injured employees, and checks occupational safety and health policies of the organization for compliance with federal, state, and local regulations.

In order to prevent electrocution of an employee, you may be required to check the possible hazards in all the electrical outlets. A responsible job? What do you think?

Employee and Labor Relations

The power of employees as individuals to bargain with their employer and to protect themselves from arbitrary or unfair treatment is limited. Because of this, many employees find it to their advantage to bargain collectively with their employer through a union.

Personnel workers in employee and labor relations have principal responsibility for collective bargaining, preparation for contract negotiations and administration, and grievance settlement, as well as preparation for arbitration.

The personnel worker is asked to consult with company executives and supervisors when they contemplate taking action that will almost certainly result in unfavorable employee reaction. Consider, for example, what is likely to happen when the sales of one of the company's products have declined, with the result that a backlog of inventory has accumulated and made it necessary to lay off those employees engaged in the production of the overstocked item. Surely this will have an adverse effect upon workers suddenly thrown out of jobs, as well as upon the morale of those still employed. Repercussions can be minimized, however, if the layoff is preceded by a careful study of the situation.

How many of those whose jobs are affected can be put to work temporarily elsewhere in the plant? Will the employees thus transferred receive their usual compensation or the rate of pay for the jobs to which they are assigned during the layoff? How will the company select the ones to be laid off? Will only those go who have been with the company for a short time, or will old-timers go? Will layoff time be added to length-of-service credits (which help determine the amount of vacation time, pension, and other benefits to which an employee is entitled), or will these credits not be permitted to accumulate for laid off workers while they are gone? Since there are several holidays, like Christmas and Fourth of July, for which employees customarily are paid without working, will those laid off be compensated for holidays that occur during the layoff? Will each worker be notified when to return to work, or must the employee "check in" occasionally to find out? Will the company try to help those affected find work with other employers during the layoff?

The employee relations worker is expected to know, or sense, that these and perhaps other questions will be on the employees' minds. He or she may be given the responsibility of composing a written notice that explains the reason for layoff and answers the questions before they are asked. This carefully prepared explanation, signed by the production department head and posted on the bulletin boards throughout the plant, will help to alleviate the blow. It will have a salutary effect upon employees who are retained but who, without such an explanation, might assume they would be the next to go. In addition it will do much to hold the goodwill of workers the company will want back when the time comes for resumption of normal production.

Often a trained personnel worker will foresee bad worker reaction when others in management, less attuned to employee thinking, do not. One corporation, looking forward to expansion, announced that it had acquired land for a new plant to be located some distance from the old one. Management thought this would be greeted with enthusiasm, but it was not. Employees were upset, assuming that the new facilities would replace the old, and mean loss of their jobs. Production tapered off. It resumed, however, when—belatedly—workers learned the facts. Had the personnel department been consulted before the announcement was written, it would have been made clear that the new plant would not affect current employees but would mean further hiring. And there would have been no loss in production!

Typical titles for this personnel worker are director of industrial relations, manager of labor relations, labor relations director, employee relations manager.

This worker's principal duties include representing the company in collective bargaining negotiations and arbitration hearings, preparing briefs and exhibits for use in negotiations or arbitration, possibly approving final contract at close of negotiations, interpreting contract provisions to all levels of management, dealing with union representatives on matters of contract interpretation and administration, and representing the company in the grievance procedure. This worker also participates with management in formulating labor relations policies, reviews industrial relations policies and practices for compliance with federal and state labor laws, sometimes prepares and distributes handbooks and manuals explaining clauses in collective bargaining agreements, assembles and analyzes information on trends in labor relations, and prepares studies on personnel problems dealing with seniority, layoff procedures, and related subjects.

If you are assigned a position in the labor relations section, your duties will be viewed by others as being extremely important and responsible. You may be called upon to brief the management negotiating team on any one of a number of vitally important subjects. You might be expected to extract from the latest area wage survey the data relevant to the occupational skills employed by your firm. You will have to be up to date on inflation and wage trends in the industry and in the community.

If employees are not unionized, the employer's personnel policies and practices can affect employee desires to unionize. Every employer, therefore, must be concerned with unions either because of the need to negotiate with them or because there is always the possibility that employees may decide to unionize.

But, unionized or not, there are many facets of dealing with the work force as a whole that come under the heading of employee and labor relations. Under the pressures of today's social forces, most employers find it advisable to treat all their employees with the same consideration they would apply if the work force were unionized. Most of the comments that follow in this section relate to unionized workers, but they might apply equally to a nonunionized work force.

A major function of a union is to negotiate and administer the labor agreement that covers the conditions of employment for its members with their employer.[12] Its function also is to protect members from unfair treatment and to assist them in resolving grievances they believe may exist in connection with their employment. By providing employees with a sense of security, power, and importance in their relations with managers, a union can exert a significant influence upon management.

Impact of the Union upon the Employer. When a union is recognized and certified as the bargaining agent for employees, an employer will have to use time that was previously devoted to other personnel functions to negotiate the labor agreement and discuss with union representatives the problems and grievances relating to its administration. Accurate personnel and financial

---

[12] Sherman, Bohlander, and Chruden. *Managing Human Resources*, 391.

records also are necessary to support the company's position during contract negotiations or grievance hearings. Wages, hours, and conditions of work are, by law, all proper subjects for collective bargaining between management and the union. In keeping with current trends in personnel management, unions typically seek to achieve participation in those company decisions that affect the employment, security, and welfare of their members.

Appeal of the Union. Identification with the union can give the employees an added feeling of security and equality in relations with their boss. As members of a union, they need have less hesitation in challenging those actions of their employer with which they disagree or in expressing their sentiments freely about their jobs since they know that the union is obligated to provide protection from possible retaliatory action.

Among the benefits to union members are the economic ones that the union can offer its membership. By bargaining collectively with an employer, workers have far greater strength than they would ever have as individuals in their demands for higher wages, improved fringe benefits, greater job security, and a shorter work week.

Union Leadership. To interpret the behavior of union leaders, one must understand their backgrounds and ambitions and recognize the political aspects of the offices they occupy. The leaders in many of the national unions have developed political machines that enable them to suppress opposition and to perpetuate themselves in office. Tenure in office for the leader in a local union, however, is less secure. In the local union, officers periodically must run for reelection, and if they are to remain in office, they must be able to convince a majority of the members that they are serving them effectively.

Some unions recognize that the practice of obtaining leaders from the ranks can serve to weaken the organization. Therefore, they bring in persons with advanced education to become union officers rather than just employed staff specialists.

Government Regulation of Labor Relations. Relations between the union and the employer are governed by state and federal laws. These laws evolved from common law and legislation and from legal interpretations rendered by the National Labor Relations Board and the courts. Contemporary interest in labor legislation is centered on three specific acts of federal legislation.

The Wagner Act. The essence of the act is contained in Section 7, providing employee bargaining rights as follows:

> Employees shall have the right to self-organization, to form, join, or assist labor organizations, to bargain collectively through representatives of their own choosing, and to engage in concerted activities, for the purpose of collective bargaining or other mutual aid or protection....

Other provisions of the Wagner Act stipulate unfair labor practices on the part of employers. In addition, the Wagner Act provided for the establishment of the National Labor Relations Board to consider cases brought before it.

The Taft-Hartley Act. The Taft-Hartley Act modified some of the provisions of the Wagner Act. Primarily, though, it lists those actions on the part of unions that are considered unfair labor practices. One of the major effects of the Act was to relax the restrictions that the Wagner Act had placed upon an employer's freedom of speech. The Act also increased the conditions under which court injunctions might be issued in labor disputes, as well as the opportunities to obtain court injunctions against certain illegal strikes and other unfair practices by the unions.

The Landrum-Griffin Act. One of the most important provisions of the act is the bill of rights for union members which requires that every union member must be given the right to nominate candidates for union office, vote in union elections, attend union meetings, participate in union meetings, and vote on union business. Another provision of the act establishes certain ground rules governing the use of members within the trusteed locals. Additionally, an important provision concerns the reports that unions and employers are required to submit, including financial reports of the operation of the union.

Current Labor Issues. The many conflicts and strains that are occurring within this nation's social structure are having a significant effect upon union policies and practices and upon the attitudes and behavior of their members. Union problems resulting from today's rapidly occurring social, economic, and technological trends are very different from those that confronted unions when they were in their formative years.

Changing character of the union member. In the early days of the labor movement, unions tended to consist of members who knew firsthand what employment conditions could be like without unions and what personal sacrifices were required to organize and make a union survive. As subsequent generations entered the unions, their memberships have contained fewer individuals who are dedicated to the social causes of the unions. Furthermore, union members no longer may be categorized as being from a downtrodden working class, but rather they are identified with the American middle class.

Unions and civil rights. The gains achieved by organized labor have helped to plant the seeds of some very significant problems for both unions and their leaders in the area of civil rights. Members of black and other protected groups have become frustrated because they believe that they have not been accorded fair, equal opportunity to participate in the gains being realized by organized labor as a whole. Frustration over alleged injustices by unions, whether real or perceived, has led to militant actions by black labor leaders aimed at increasing black leadership control in labor organizations and in enlarging the membership and employment of black workers in the crafts and other jobs with higher pay.

Unionization of white collar groups. Traditionally, white-collar employees tended to identify themselves with the owners or managers and to perform similar work activities in proximity with them. As a group, they enjoyed certain privileges and socioeconomic status that blue collar workers did not have.

In recent years, however, growth in the size of organizations in which white collar groups are employed has tended to impersonalize their work and to isolate them from and reduce their identification with management. The lack of job security during layoffs resulting from automation or declining sales, together with growing difficulties encountered in attempting to resolve grievances, have helped to push them toward unionization.

Collective Bargaining. Employer recognition of a union constitutes the first stage in the establishment of a bargaining relationship. Such recognition often is the result of a unionizing campaign initiated either by employees with the organization, by an outside union acting on its own, or at the invitation of the employees. The success or failure of an organizing campaign depends largely on the working climate and morale that exists within the employer's organization.

Recognition Procedures. Union elections are usually conducted by the National Labor Relations Board. Ballots permit the employees the choice of "no union" as well as the names of the contending unions. The union receiving a majority of the votes is certified by the NLRB as the bargaining agent for a period of at least a year or for the duration of the labor agreement.

Recognition gives a union the right to represent employees within a particular bargaining unit that may or may not encompass the entire organization. The bargaining unit may be defined as a group of employees recognized by an employer or designated by an agency as appropriate for representation by employee organization for purposes of bargaining. The key factor in considering the composition of the bargaining unit is the basis of common occupational interest.

Negotiations. After recognition is achieved, the parties must get together for the purpose of negotiations. Collective bargaining is the process by which the employer and the union negotiate the conditions under which the members within the bargaining unit are to be employed. These conditions are described in the labor agreement that results from such bargaining.

In the bargaining process sometimes negotiations break down. Then the union may try to bring pressure to bear on management to meet its demands. Several tactics are available to the union.

Strike. A strike involves the refusal of a group of employees to perform their jobs. It is the withholding of services of that part of the work force on strike.

Picketing. When a union goes on strike, it is general practice for the union to picket the employer by placing persons at the entrances to the premises to advertise the dispute and to discourage persons from entering or leaving these premises. A picket line can result in the refusal by employees of other organizations to cross the picket line to deliver and pick up goods.

Boycotting. Another economic weapon of unions is the boycott. This results when a union refuses to allow its members to patronize a business enterprise where there is a labor dispute.

Lockout. Under special circumstances, when labor and management cannot come to agreement, management may choose to lock its workers out. This is done by simply shutting down the plant or place of business.

Overcoming Deadlocks. When labor negotiations are deadlocked, that is, the parties cannot come to agreement, a third party may be called in so that agreement can be reached. There are several degrees of participation by third parties involved.

Conciliation. A conciliator provides a catalytic service by keeping the negotiations moving and thus helping the two parties arrive at their own solution. No attempt is made by the conciliator to impose solutions or force compromises. The effective conciliator simply keeps the talks going until the parties eventually reach solutions.

Mediator. A mediator exercises a more positive role in helping to resolve a deadlock by suggesting compromises, solutions, or making suggestions that will lead to agreement. Both the conciliator and the mediator help the principals retreat from their deadlocked positions without suffering a loss of face. Actually, there is little difference between conciliation and mediation.

Arbitration. In arbitration both parties to the dispute agree to permit an impartial umpire or arbitrator to consider the relative merits of their respective positions and resolve the dispute through the award that the arbitrator makes for the case. The decision or award is binding on both parties.

Fact-finding. Government pressure may be exerted in some circumstances through the appointment of a fact-finding board to investigate a bargaining deadlock. The board has no power, but it can make public its findings thus bringing pressure to bear on the principals to the dispute.

The Labor Agreement. After agreement has been reached through collective bargaining, it is put in writing and signed by the representatives of both parties. The major portion of the agreement is concerned with conditions of employment. These conditions include wages, hours, fringe benefits, and various provisions covering discipline and other personnel actions.

In the negotiating process, management strives to preserve its rights or prerogatives. In a sense, management's authority is supreme in all matters except those it has expressly conceded in the collective bargaining agreement or in those areas where its authority is restricted by law. The inclusion of a management's rights clause in the work agreement represents a "no trespassing" notice that the employer hopes will deter the union from encroaching on its exclusive territory.

Union security is as important to the union as management rights are to the employer. Union security determines the extent to which the jobs within its representation area will be held by the union members and the extent to which the union will be able to maintain disciplinary control over members. Within these provisions are the various degrees of security determined by the kind of shop agreed upon in the work agreement.

The union shop provides that any person who is hired, if not a union member at the time, must join the union within a prescribed period—usually thirty days—as a condition of employment. The agency shop does not require employees in the bargaining unit to join the union, but it does require that they pay dues to the union that serves as their bargaining agent within the organization. The closed shop requires that an employer hire only those who are union members. Additionally, under a checkoff provision the employer withholds the union dues from the paycheck of each union member who signs an affidavit agreeing to such a deduction.

Employee Grievances. No matter how carefully and conscientiously the union and the employer may negotiate the labor agreement, differences over its administration and application are almost certain to arise between the two parties. Typically, union grievances are a response to actions that it believes the employer has taken or failed to take in living up to the terms of the labor agreement or the policies of the organization.

Grievances can result from a variety of causes. Many of them involve the agreement and result from omissions or ambiguities in its provisions that cause each party to interpret differently the meaning of a particular provision or how a particular personnel decision should be made. Sometimes grievances stem from a failure of employees either to meet the demands of their jobs or to gain satisfaction from performing them, or both. Employees who are placed in the wrong job, for instance, are more likely to perform unsatisfactorily. Another source of grievance lies in supervisory practices. The supervisor's attitude and behavior toward individual workers and the union may provide a fertile source of grievances.

Most large organizations have formal grievance procedures that provide for an airing of the grievance and consideration of it at various levels of the organization until the grievant is satisfied or the solution sought is finally denied. In a unionized shop, it is the union officer, such as the steward, or the grievance committee that will represent the interest of the aggrieved worker. Management is represented in these discussions by, first, the first-line supervisor, then probably the company personnel officer, then finally someone at the top management level such as the general manager or the president of the firm.

If a solution is not forthcoming within the structure of the grievance procedure as provided, the union has two alternative courses of action if it wishes to pursue the matter further. It can call a strike, or it can submit the grievance to arbitration. Most grievances are settled at the first level between the worker, the supervisor, and the union steward in the shop.

Disciplinary Action. The purpose of a disciplinary program is to provide the means for securing employee performance and behavior that is necessary to meet organizational goals. While one of its purposes is to provide corrective action, a more important purpose is to prevent the need for such action in the first place.

Definite policies and procedures for handling disciplinary matters are essential for ensuring fair treatment of offenders. While it is usually recommended that disciplinary action be handled on an impartial basis without regard for the specific circumstances involved, most individuals rebel against the imposition of inflexible rules.

Before taking any disciplinary action, supervisors should interview the employees with a view to obtaining the reasons for their behaviors and attitudes and any information that will enable the supervisors to understand the infraction. A record of offenses and disciplinary action taken is usually maintained in the employee's personnel file. Supervisors must be able to distinguish between what does and does not constitute a valid disciplinary case. Furthermore, they must learn how to document their case against an employee so that the evidence supporting their action will not be refuted by evidence that the union presents in the arbitration hearing. In considering the facts in a disciplinary case, the arbitrator or other person hearing the appeal usually will seek to determine the extent, if any, to which the disciplined employee was at fault and the extent, if any, to which management may also have been at fault.

Any necessary disciplinary actions should be administered only after the case has been reviewed thoroughly to ensure that the individual being disciplined is completely responsible for her or his actions, that every possible effort has been made to make the employee aware of the deficiency and what is expected, and that he or she is being counseled in order to improve performance and behavior. Not only will the respect of the employees and the union be increased by the proper handling of disciplinary problems, but also any action that is taken is less likely to be reversed subsequently through the grievance procedure or through arbitration.

Personnel Research[13]

The duties of this section are to collect and analyze all kinds of data related to personnel and employment, including numbers of personnel, wage levels and trends, human resources planning needs, and new developments in the field.

Most progressive personnel departments are continually conducting at least some research on such problems as accident proneness and causes of absenteeism and on such subjects as employer-employee communication, wage incentives, and the most effective methods of utilizing the services of the physically handicapped. These studies help to determine personnel policy. Sometimes they are carried on by full-time researchers.

The typical title for this individual is director of personnel research.

The principal duties of the director of personnel research are to conduct systematic investigations into current personnel problems of the organization; to investigate new and improved methods of management including testing, training, compensating, and other functions; and to maintain records of employment and investigate indications of increasing turnover rates.

If the turnover rate in the purchasing department has sud-

---

[13] Yoder and Staudohar, *Personnel Management*, 516-525.

denly increased, that bears looking into, and the director of research conducts an investigation in conjunction with the purchasing officer.

Research can be defined as systematic and purposeful investigation of facts with the object of determining cause and effect relationships among such facts. From research we hope to establish principles that define the relationship between two or more phenomena. Managers then attempt to use these principles in their philosophy, approach, attitude, and specific practices.

Two general types of research are usually identified as basic or exploratory and operational or applied. Exploratory research is concerned with the discovery of knowledge for its own sake. The scientist builds conceptual models and tests various hypotheses against them. Operational or applied research is directed toward the solution of particular business problems. The payoff of operational or applied research is immediate, observable, and tangible.

A wide variety of people and institutions engage in either pure or applied research. Some of these are described below.

Colleges and Universities. These institutions are set up to operate at both the pure and applied levels of personnel research. It is common to see bureaus of business research that engage in personnel projects as well as investigations in other fields of business management. Among the outstanding university centers of personnel research are the Institute for Social Research of the University of Michigan, Personnel Research Board of Ohio State University, Institute of Industrial Relations of the University of California, the Behavioral Sciences Group of Carnegie Institute of Technology, and the Center for Industrial Relations of the University of Minnesota.

Government Agencies. Various governmental agencies conduct basic and applied research. Units of the U.S. Department of Labor are particularly interested in research dealing with personnel management. For example, the *Dictionary of Occupational Titles* was prepared by the United States Employment Service for the general use of industry.

Private Research Organizations. These organizations take a number of different forms. Some are employers' associations that accomplish particular projects of special interest to an industry. For example, industry wage and salary surveys may be conducted by an employers' association on a continuing basis. In addition, there are the larger employer groups like National Association of Manufacturers and the Chamber of Commerce of the United States. Other associations are established strictly for the purpose of conducting business research. Such organizations as the Conference Board, the RAND Corporation, and the Stanford Research Institute are examples.

Individual Companies. Individual companies also do personnel research, particularly of the operational or applied type.

Research Methods. All research involves the application, in some manner, of the scientific method. There are various specific forms that individual research projects can take.

Controlled experiments. Controlled experiments conducted by private concerns are relatively rare. Perhaps the most famous experiment of this type was the Hawthorne study of the Western Electric Company, begun in 1927. In this experiment the work force was divided into two groups, experimental and control. In the experimental group, there was an attempt to keep extraneous variables constant and then to introduce one variation into the situation. The resulting acts could then be attributed to the single variant factor. In this manner changes that sought to improve lighting, rest periods, and air conditioning showed immediate results in terms of improved productivity. No similar results were observed in the control group. To validate the discovered relationships, the conditions were returned to their original status in the expectation that productivity would drop. To everyone's great surprise, productivity did not drop and in some instances continued to improve. Obviously the conditions of the experiment had not been rigidly controlled. In personnel research it is impossible to keep all other factors constant and then isolate them one at a time. What was not controlled were the minds and attitudes of the participating workers. They liked

Figure 2-1

ORGANIZATION CHART
Human Resources Division of a Major Industrial Organization

VICE PRESIDENT FOR HUMAN RESOURCES

DIRECTOR OF PERSONNEL RELATIONS

Employment and Placement

- Human resources planning
- Recruiting
- Interviewing
- Testing
- Reference checks
- Hiring
- Placement
- Orientation
- Transfer
- Promotion
- Termination
- Record keeping
- Equal opportunity
- Affirmative action
- Staffing research

Wage and Salary Administration

- Compensation planning
- Wage adminis-tration
- Salary adminis-tration
- Overtime pay
- Wage incentive
- Bonus payments
- Profit sharing
- Wage surveys
- Job evaluation
- Position classification
- Performance appraisal
- Executive compensation
- Job enrichment
- Compensation research

Training and Development

- Operative training
- Supervisor training
- Manager development
- Advancement consideration
- Training research
- Development counseling
- Relations with schools and colleges

Employee Benefits and Services

- Vacations credits
- Sick leave
- Health insurance
- Worker's compensation
- Disability insurance
- Unemployment insurance
- Employee counseling
- Retirement plan
- Suggestion system
- Employee facilities
- Food service
- Veteran's Administration
- Social Security matters
- Publications

DIRECTOR OF LABOR RELATIONS

Safety and Health	Research	Employee and Labor Relations
Occupation safety and health matters Safety and health standards Compliance inspection Report injuries On-site treatment Safety and health inspections Physical exams First aid Accident prevention Plant security	Collect data Analyze data Investigate problems Investigate new management methods Maintain liaison with other research organizations Keep appraised of new developments in personnel management and techniques	Preparation for negotiations Contract negotiations Contract administration Grievance processing Legislative analysis Employee relations Preparation for grievances, legal actions, compensation claims Arbitration

working in the experimental group; they felt very important. Regardless of what was done to them, they attempted to produce more. Recognition of the importance of these personnel resulted in marked increases in the productivity.

Surveys. The survey is a commonly used research method. It usually takes the form of a questionnaire or structured interview. Its object is to determine present practices or approaches and to attempt to relate certain results to particular causes. For example, we may wish to know certain things about employee profit sharing. Can such plans survive a profitless year? If so, how many profitless years? Certain hypotheses must be established around which survey questions can be phrased. What criteria can be established so that we can judge the correctness of such hypotheses? When the actual survey is taken, companies are asked questions concerning the possible causes of the absence of profits. As a result, certain generalizations deducible from the study can be made.

Historical studies. There is a wealth of useful information in the files of most firms, including valuable records about personnel. Suppose, for example, that a manager wishes to do research on a problem of high labor turnover. The manager can study turnover experience on the basis of such variables as sex, age, department, home ownership, marital status, and stated causes for leaving.

Case studies. The case study approach is considered by many to be a separate method of research. Quite frequently, however, case studies result only in the creation of further hypotheses requiring additional research to validate. Case studies are intensive in that a great number of subjects is investigated in detail in a relatively limited number of firms.

Simulation. In recent years, simulation of performance has become an increasingly popular method of research in many fields. Simulations have been used in business environments for studying problems of production control, inventory control, purchasing, and marketing.

Systematic and purposeful research is an obvious and continuing necessity in the field of personnel management. The future is never certain, but on the basis of an analysis of present trends, we can foresee certain events in the field of personnel management. Among them we can anticipate (1) a continuing emphasis upon human relations, with a switch to an emphasis upon creativity and productivity as contrasted with happiness and satisfaction; (2) a greater role in helping to meet the private business firm's broader responsibility to society; (3) expansion of the field of personnel management to include organizational planning for growth; (4) an increasing acceptance of the responsibility for effective personnel management on the part of all managers; and (5) a marked effort on the part of the personnel manager to assist the organization and its members to adjust to the inevitability of automated processes. The most dynamic element of our business economy is people. The expert in people, the personnel manager, has both an opportunity and a challenge in the business management of the future.

PERSONNEL RECORDS

An indispensable feature of every personnel department is its personnel records file. This is a complete record of each employee's history with the organization, starting with the employment application. It includes such data as factors that the medical department indicates might have an effect upon the individual's employment, the worker's salary or wage record, a compilation of the jobs an individual has held, a history of the employee's attendance and tardiness, any work-related accidents, and accounts of any disciplinary difficulties the employee may have experienced. Personnel records are confidential and not permitted to leave the employee relations department. They are referred to constantly for a variety of purposes, but only by authorized people. Computers are now used to store, retrieve, and print out all or selected items of personnel information.

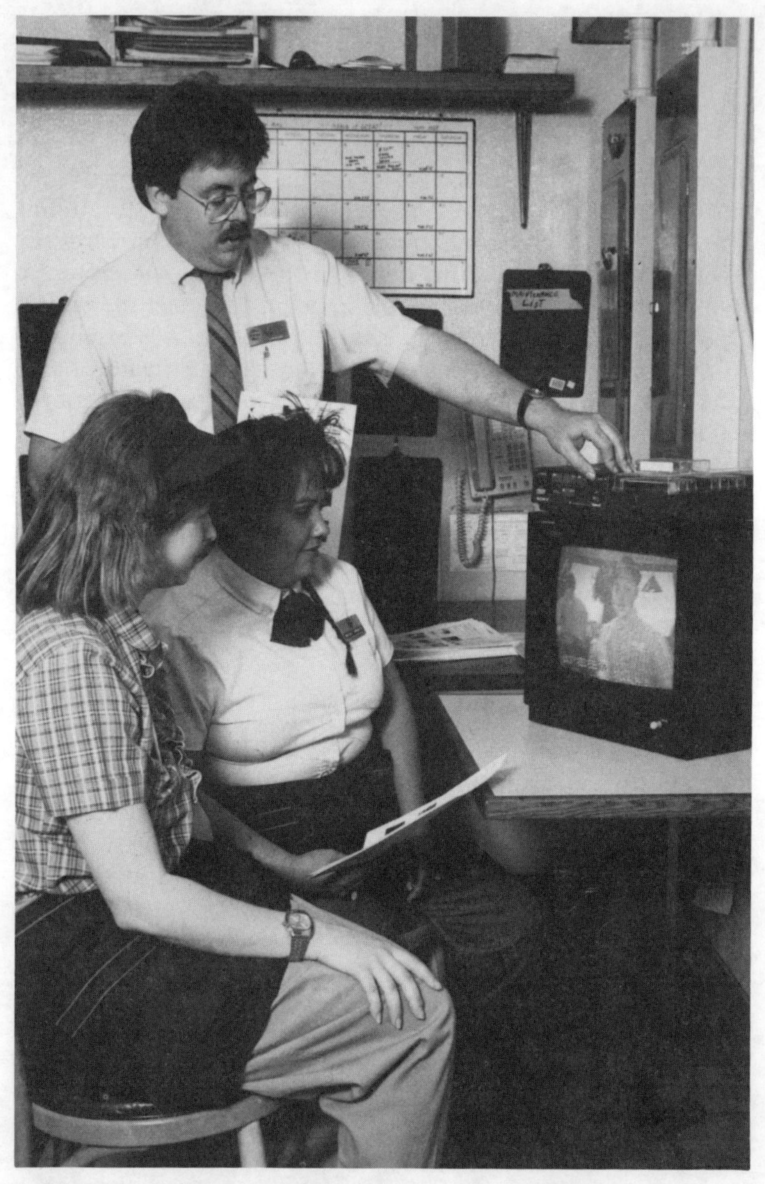

Training new employees to perform their jobs well is an important part of human resources work. (Pizza Hut photo)

CHAPTER 3

CHARACTERISTICS OF THE OCCUPATION

All personnel/human resources managers perform common management functions including planning the objectives and programs of the personnel department, organizing the work to be done, and filling the positions needed to perform the work. They also direct the efforts of the division of human resources by controlling the work activities, reviewing performance, and taking necessary corrective action.

SALARIES

Salaries in the field of human resources differ a great deal from one position to another. Factors causing variations include the size of the firm, level of responsibility, length of service, locality, and the nature of the organization. Because job titles are far from uniform, and because a position described as *personnel manager* in one enterprise might be called *director of human resources* in another, specific salaries by job can only be described in terms of averages or ranges. The following tables list the titles most commonly used in human resources departments and show the average salaries for each.

Table 3-1. Human Resources Job Titles and Salaries, 1987

Job Titles	*Pvt. Sector – Average*	*Federal Govt – Range*
Personnel Clerk	$14,310	$11,802-15,339
Personnel Specialist	22,207	16,521-21,480
Human Resources Technician	40,229	27,172-35,326
Human Resources Manager	65,106	38,727-50,346
Human Resources Executive	78,123	45,763-59,488

Source: U.S. Department of Labor. Bureau of Labor Statistics. *National Survey of Professional, Administrative, Technical, and Clerical Pay: Private Service Industries.* Bulletin 2290. Washington: Government Printing Office, 1987.

The 1988 Human Resource Compensation Survey released in June 1988 by the American Society for Personnel Administration and William M. Mercer-Meidinger-Hansen Inc., highlights some very interesting and pertinent data concerning salaries and compensation (compensation = salary + bonus) for human resource management personnel.[14] Some of these data are shown in Table 3-2.

Although the total compensations of top human resources executives are not reflected in these tables, the survey did include the following information:

- Top human resources executives receive approximately the same bonus levels as top marketing executives, top engineering executives, and corporate treasurers.
- Average total compensation (salary plus bonus) was over $100,000 for top human resource management executives.

---

[14] McMillan, John D. and Claire O. Walters. "Dominating the Dollars." *Personnel Administrator.* American Society for Personnel Administration, August 1988.

- Thirty percent of all top human resource management executives reported a base salary of over $100,000.
- The average bonus for all top human resource incumbents was over $28,000.

Table 3-2. Salaries for Human Resource Specialties

Newer Specialties

Manager Level	*Average Salary $44,200*
Human Resources Information Systems Manager	$44,100
Employee Assistance Programs Manager	44,300
Professional Level	*Average Salary $33,600*
Human Resources Information Systems Specialist	$32,900
Employee Assistance Programs Counselor	34,200

Representative Established Specialties

Manager Level	*Average Salary $46,900*
Compensation Manager	$49,700
Benefits Manager	50,300
Equal Employment Opportunity Manager	48,600
Recruiting Manager	43,600
Training Manager	42,200
Professional Level	*Average Salary $29,600*
Compensation Analyst	$27,900
Benefits Administrator	29,900
Training Specialist	31,600
Equal Employment Opportunity Specialist	32,900
Recruiter	25,500

Where the Salaries Are

The following lists indicate the average salaries of top human resource management executives according to location, industry, and size of employment.[15]

By Location:

New York City	$110,000
Los Angeles	93,000
Washington, D.C.	74,800
Atlanta	92,400
Chicago	96,800
Boston	90,500
Minneapolis	84,000
Philadelphia	89,600
Dallas	94,100

By Industry:

Manufacturing/non-durable	$103,400
Manufacturing/durable	92,000
Wholesale/retail trade	96,400
Finance	82,200
Insurance	78,800
Services for profit	88,200
Utilities	84,800

[15] Ropp, Kirkland. "HR Management for All It's Worth." *Personnel Administrator.* September 1987. Derived from ASPA/Hansen 1987 Human Resource Management Compensation Survey, February 1987. American Society for Personnel Administration.

By Employment Size:	
Over 10,000	$117,000
3,500-10,000	94,000
1,300-3,500	80,800
650-1,300	77,200
250-650	76,800
Under 250	73,100

WORKING CONDITIONS

Employees in personnel offices generally work about forty hours a week.[16] During periods of intensive recruitment or emergency, they may work much longer. As a rule, they are paid for holidays and vacations and share in retirement plans, life and health insurance plans, and other benefits available to all professional workers in their organizations.

Working conditions for personnel workers are generally very favorable. The offices are usually well lighted, ventilated, and pleasant places in which to work.

Personnel workers meet and work with all types of people—job applicants, union representatives, local officials of the community, educators, and other community groups and company executives. They may address meetings held with the firm's employees, supervisors, or civic groups.

SATISFACTIONS

There are many personal and professional satisfactions to be derived from working in the field of personnel/human

---

[16] *Occupational Outlook Handbook*, 1988-89, 40.

resources. Particular aspects of the work may well have more meaning for some, but every personnel worker finds most of the work very rewarding.

Personnel work is basically office work, located close to management. There is a complexity to the work that adds to the challenge of the assignment. It is brain work rather than manual labor and requires intellectual rather than physical effort.

Personnel assignments provide a professional status. Professional jobs require responsibility and specialized technical training. The recognition on the part of others of the responsibility of the job gives status to the position.

Personnel workers derive psychological rewards from the degree of professionalism of the work and the long-range improvements they are able to accomplish for the good of the organization, its employees, and the community. Social satisfaction also may be derived from the extent of human relations involved in the assignment. The wide range of personal contacts —with managers, supervisors, and individual employees—and the opportunity to be helpful to all of them are sources of social satisfaction.

The broad field of human resources is open to new applications of developing technologies. For example, electronic data processing is now widely used in personnel recordkeeping.

It is satisfying to know that salaries paid workers in human resources management equal or exceed other comparable fields. Personnel workers are now receiving monetary recognition for their responsibilities and efforts.

WORKING LEVELS

The organizational structure of a large industry may be considered as comprising five levels of personnel workers. These levels are clerical, specialist, technical, managerial, and executive. The first two are white collar, hourly wage employees. The others represent three different levels within the management structure of the organization.

The personnel functions as performed at each level of the organization are described below in the following terms: duties, wages/salaries, conditions, hours, and satisfactions. The comments are generalized for broad application.

Clerical Level

The clerical is the lowest level employed in the personnel office. It is the beginning level for white collar workers in the occupational field of human resources management.

Duties. If you were a personnel worker at the clerical level, you would be engaged in the usual office tasks such as typing, filing, phoning, and other typical work. In a personnel office these tasks would be related to maintaining personnel files, processing papers, compiling lists, and digging out information related to organization employees in the personnel files.

Wages/Salaries. The current federal minimum wage is $3.35 per hour. As a beginning clerical worker you could expect this wage or a little more at the start. With time and demonstrated proficiency, you could expect some increases in wages on a periodic basis.

Conditions. As a personnel worker, you would usually work in an office that is well lighted, ventilated, and pleasant. Until familiar with the work of the office and the rules governing the personnel processes, you can't expect to do much other than the routine paperwork. As you gain experience and knowledge of the processes of personnel administration, your assignments may be broadened to include more contact with applicants and others who come into the office for assistance.

Hours. You will probably work an eight-hour day, forty-hour week. Some firms are shifting to four ten-hour days per week. Most personnel offices are open by eight o'clock in the morning and remain open until five or six in the afternoon. This usually means there will be some staggering of the work shift to have the office continually staffed during the day. You may have to work the second, or swing, shift in order to process time cards of the day shift or other pay and time-related matters.

Satisfactions. At the clerical level you will derive satisfaction from learning more about the job and the importance of carrying out your duties with accuracy. You will also feel satisfaction from the growing skills you develop as you carry out the duties of your assignments. When you get to know your colleagues and feel comfortable in the work place, you will feel more a part of the work force.

Specialist Level

Workers at this level are experienced in personnel work. They are white collar workers—wage earners who have worked for a considerable time and developed skills in which they have become specialized. They perform a special function in this regard. Examples include interviewers, testers, and benefits counselors.

Duties. At the specialist level you will have accumulated a thorough working knowledge of all the personnel processes, rules, and regulations. You will perform duties requiring a knowledge of terms and usage of personnel information. Also you may extract information from a variety of sources and combine data in ways that are useful to the office in the compilation of reports and other applications. At this level, you will be expected to operate a computer terminal.

As a specialist you may have a number of clerical level helpers. You will probably perform many duties under some supervision, such as interviewing, counseling employees on benefits, and preparing reports.

Wages/Salaries. An experienced personnel worker at the specialist level can expect $22,000 per year or more. Variations from this amount will depend on the size of the organization, pay scale, amount of experience, extent of responsibilities, time on the job, and other factors. As a personnel specialist you are a very valuable employee who contributes much to the satisfaction of the work force.

Conditions. Your working conditions are the same as for all personnel workers. As a specialist, however, you may require a semiprivate office or location in order to conduct interviews, counsel, or perform other tasks requiring freedom from noise and interruption.

Hours. You will probably have to observe the same hours as other white collar workers, the standard forty-hour week. At peak periods of the year, some paid overtime may be involved.

Satisfactions. At the specialist level you will find satisfaction in being able to perform those services that meet the needs of the office and the individual employee who comes to you for assistance. Frequently you will be the one who keeps the routine of the office functioning smoothly. The management of the office and the organization depend on you for special treatment of data and other information and functions that you are peculiarly able to provide.

Technical Level

Work at the technical level involves those duties usually associated with the first line of supervision. The technical level is the lower level of management in the occupational field of personnel/human resources.

Duties. As a relatively new personnel manager you may serve in the capacity of a personnel technician. The title *personnel analyst* is frequently used in connection with positions at this level. You might head up a technical section of the human resources office such as the training section.

Job analyst is a typical technical title. Also called compensation analysts, they do very exacting work. They collect and examine detailed information about job duties in order to prepare job descriptions. These descriptions or "position classifications" explain the duties, training, and skills each job requires. Whenever a large organization introduces a new job or reviews existing ones, it calls upon the expert knowledge of the job analyst. Accurate information about job duties also is required when an organization considers changes in its pay system.

Wages/Salaries. At this level, you will be salaried. That means that you are not paid by the hour, but rather are paid on the basis of doing a particular kind of work and carrying out the duties assigned. You may receive salary increases on a periodic basis. The reward for doing a job very well is not so much an increase in pay, but rather improved chances for promotion when the opportunity arises. Current salaries are approximately $34,000 per year.

Conditions. Working conditions for technicians in personnel will be comfortable, but probably not spacious. You may spend a great deal of time in your office or, depending on the assignment, you may spend much time on the plant floor or in the field, investigating personnel matters.

Hours. Most managers are not restricted as to the number of hours they work. You are expected to work approximately forty hours each week, but if the job takes only thirty-five hours one week, you are not expected to sit around and twiddle your thumbs. The next week probably the work will require forty-five or fifty hours of your time. Like all young managers, you are expected to be on the job when the office opens in the morning, typically eight o'clock. You will usually stay on the job until all the principal members of the management structure in the personnel department have left for the day. One of the best ways for the novice personnel manager to learn is to spend time on the job hammering away at problems until they are solved.

Satisfactions. You and other managers at this level will derive satisfaction from solving the technical problems confronting you. It is the source of much satisfaction to see how your own efforts mesh with other technical managers and contribute to the total personnel program. There is always plenty of action for the young manager in a personnel office.

Managerial Level

This is the middle management level in the division of human resources of a large enterprise.

Duties. At the managerial level your duties encompass a

broader range than at the lower levels. You may have to direct the overall personnel program and coordinate subordinate programs, such as the training program, the benefits program, and others. At the managerial level you become involved in planning for the future direction of the enterprise as well as overseeing the subordinate programs. You may become involved in advising other managers in the organization concerning their interests in the personnel program and in the management of their personnel.

Wages/Salaries. The higher you go in the organizational structure, the more difficult it is to pin down salaries and duties. There is much variation between companies in the range of responsibilities assigned, titles utilized, and salaries paid. Directors of personnel in medium-sized firms can expect to be paid something in excess of $40,000 per year. If you head up the personnel program in a very large firm and serve under a vice president for industrial relations, you may be paid upwards from $65,000 per year. Directors of labor relations may be paid more.

Conditions. At the managerial level you can expect very comfortable working conditions. Typically you will have a well-appointed office in which you can carry on the business of the personnel program with considerable privacy. You need facilities to accommodate the other managers who will frequently be visiting the personnel director's office. A modern office may provide you with a computer terminal so you can call up information from the electronic storage file of personnel data. Some managers with a great deal of responsibility for the personnel program will not have adequate accommodations. Much depends on the view the organization holds of the personnel function and the space available to accommodate it.

Hours. At the managerial level, you can expect to work something in excess of forty hours per week. Like all managers, you are paid to get the job done. If it takes more than forty hours some weeks, that's only what is to be expected.

Satisfactions. With the current mushrooming of personnel/human resources law at the federal and state levels, there may be some satisfaction in not being hauled into court for violation of the ambiguous requirements. In reality, however, you will find there are many sources of satisfaction in being a personnel manager. A declinings glad tidings. A stable work force contributing to high productivity is a very satisfying condition. Being able to meet the challenge of changing requirements without upsetting the morale of the work force is surely a source of satisfaction.

In this occupational field we recognize that there is little standardization of titles and job responsibilities. At the managerial level the personnel manager might be titled *director of personnel* or something else. At the executive level the top personnel manager might be titled *director of personnel* or *vice president for human resources* or another term. However, the general job description that follows under the title *director of personnel* is applicable to managerial level personnel directors in very large corporations.[17]

> [Director of personnel] Directs a personnel management program for a company or a segment of a company. Serves top management officials of the organization as the source of advice and assistance on personnel management matters and problems generally: is typically consulted on the personnel implications of planned changes in management policy or program, the effects on the organization of economic or market trends, product or production method changes, etc.; represents management in contacts with other companies, trade associations, government agencies, etc., dealing primarily with personnel management matters.
>
> Typically the director of personnel for a company reports to a company officer in charge of human resources/personnel management activities or an officer of similar level. Below the company level the director of personnel typically reports to a company officer or a high management official who has responsibility for the operation of a plant, segment of the company.
>
> For a job to be covered by this definition, the personnel management program must include responsibility for all three of the following functions:

[17] *National Survey.* See note, Table 3-1.

1. *Administering a job evaluation system:* i.e., a system in which there are established procedures by which jobs are analyzed and evaluated on the basis of their duties, responsibilities, and qualification requirements in order to provide a foundation for equitable compensation. Typically, such a system includes the use of one or more sets of job evaluation factors and the preparation of formal job descriptions. It may also include such related functions as wage and salary surveys or merit rating system administration. The job evaluation system(s) does not necessarily cover all jobs in the organization, but does cover a substantial portion of the organization.
2. *Employment and placement function:* i.e., recruiting actively for at least some kinds of workers through a variety of sources (e.g., schools or colleges, employment agencies, professional societies, etc.); evaluating applicants against demands of particular jobs by use of such techniques as job analysis to determine requirements, interviews, written texts of aptitude, knowledge, or skill, reference checks, experience evaluations, etc.; recommending selections and job placements to management, etc.
3. *Employee relations and services function:* i.e., functions designed to maintain employees' morale and productivity at a high level (for example, administering a formal or informal grievance procedure; identifying and recommending solutions for personnel problems such as absenteeism, high turnover, low productivity, etc.; administration of beneficial suggestions system, retirement, pension, or insurance plans, merit rating system, etc.; overseeing cafeteria operations, recreational programs, occupational safety, and health programs, etc).

In addition, positions covered by this definition may, but do not necessarily, include responsibilities in the following areas:

- Employee training and development
- Labor relations activities
- Equal Employment Opportunity (EEO)
- Reporting under the Occupational Safety and Health Act (OSHA)

Personnel workers at the managerial level who are charged

with responsibilities related to labor relations are frequently titled *director of labor relations.* Their duties include all aspects of labor relations including collective bargaining, interpreting the work agreement, and speaking for the company at arbitration hearings.

Executive Level

This is the top management level. This is the highest level in an organization where the personnel/human resources manager serves.

Duties. This is the top level for any personnel manager with experience in any of the functional areas. Whether your title is vice president for human resources or director of personnel, as the top personnel manager in the organization you are included in the long-range planning of top management. Here you are in a position to influence company policy. You will recommend organization policy concerning personnel matters. You are a respected member of the top management team and as such you have great influence in the firm, the industry, and in the community. Your duties are so broad they will often take you away from your office.

Wages/Salaries. A recent survey made by the Bureau of Labor Statistics[18] indicates that top-level personnel directors can expect a salary in excess of $78,000 per year.

Conditions. It is safe to say that at the top level of management your working conditions are very comfortable. You will be located in the executive suite. Also, your responsibilities are very great and vital to the operation of the organization. As the top personnel executive, you will spend a great deal of your time dealing with people from outside your office and outside your organization.

Hours. At the executive level, you may be sure that you will devote many hours in excess of forty per week in carrying out

---

[18] Ibid.

the responsibilities of your assignment. Your time schedule may have enough flexibility, though, so you can get on the golf course in the middle of the week occasionally. To make up for it, you may frequently be working in the office until eight or so at night to keep up with the work, especially the volume of reading that is required at the top levels of management.

Satisfactions. As the executive level personnel manager, you will derive satisfactions from noting the progress the firm is making in terms of worker stability, low turnover rate, low accident rate, high productivity, and high morale. The major contributions you as an executive can make to your company include such things as anticipating personnel needs brought about by changes such as plant expansion. Another contribution would be the handling of labor relations to minimize labor strife at work. The strength of many a firm lies in the loyal support of a satisfied work force.

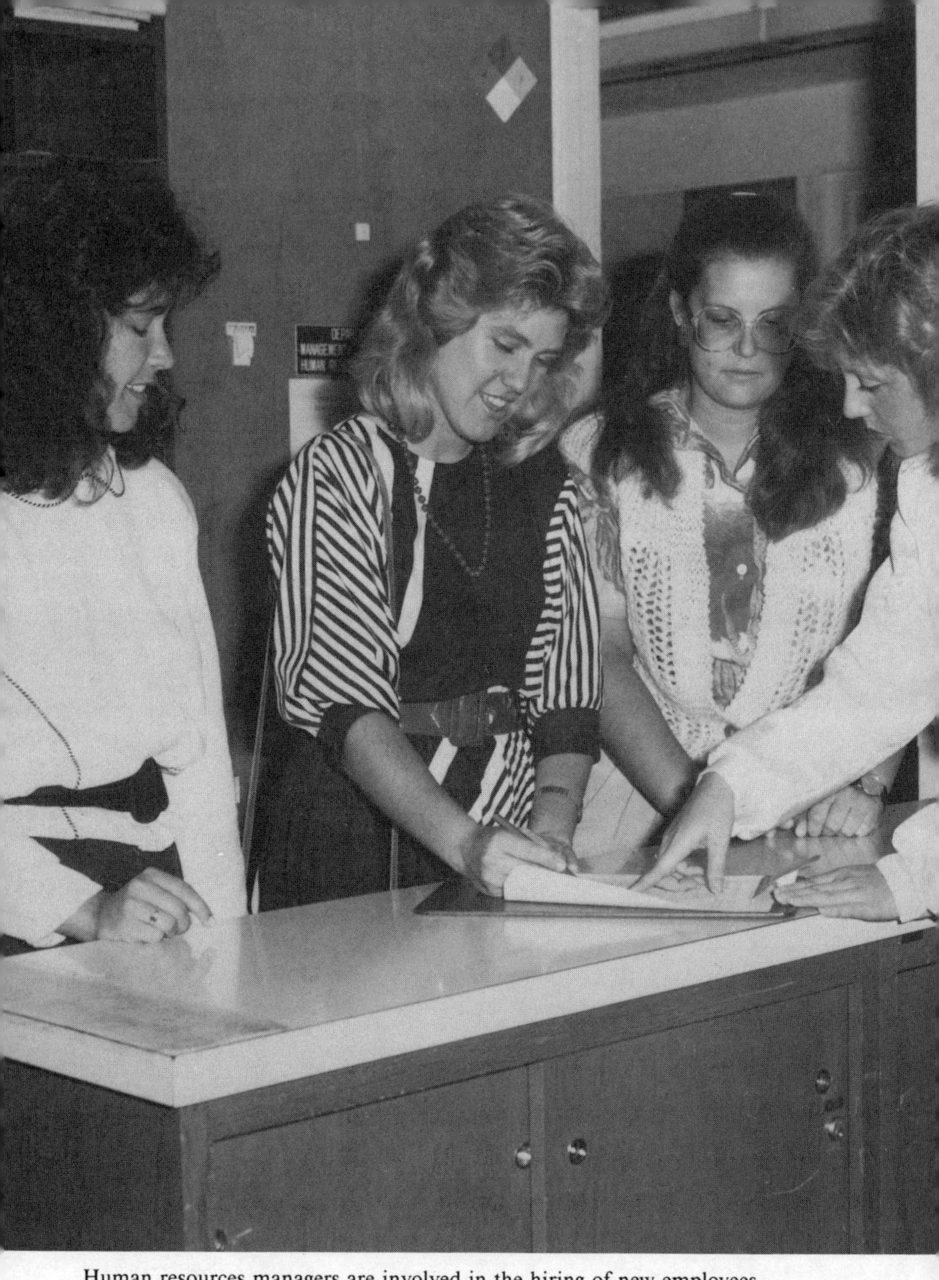

Human resources managers are involved in the hiring of new employees. (California State University, Long Beach, photo)

CHAPTER 4

QUALIFICATIONS AND PREPARATION

QUALIFICATIONS

Because of the many varied and immediate demands upon personnel workers, the work is interesting, challenging, and satisfying. It is by no means, however, suited to everyone. The duties performed by personnel workers require that they possess certain personal, professional, and educational qualifications. The most important of these are discussed below.

Personal

The personnel worker must have these basic characteristics: horse sense, love for detail, ability to understand people, a good memory, power to persuade, integrity, courage, and spiritual values. If you hope to be successful in personnel, you will need these characteristics in order to deal tactfully and patiently with others. You will be expected to speak and write well. You will have to work and communicate effectively with people possessing various degrees of intelligence and experience. The successful personnel worker will have a high tolerance for frustration.

Professional

The personnel manager needs the ability to make decisions, solve problems, move toward goals effectively, and keep in perspective the factors bearing on specific matters.

At the executive level you will need the ability to see the big picture and to translate the needs of the organization into policies, plans, programs, and actions. This includes not only the understanding of the organization internally but also the ability to catch the long-range implications of new legislation and changing public opinion.

At the managerial level you will need the ability to develop and direct programs that will carry out organization policies. You will have to be supportive of both your superiors and your subordinates.

At the technical level you, as a personnel manager, must apply your detailed knowledge to personnel programs and problems. You will implement established programs.

At the specialist level you need skills that enable you to keep several employees working smoothly. You must have thorough knowledge of personnel procedures and particular functions.

At the clerical level you'll apply skill, speed, and accuracy in typing personnel forms, maintaining personnel records, and performing general office duties. You will need to be alert and to understand directives in an environment you are just becoming accustomed to.

Educational

If you can't manage a college education, the field still is open to you. Many persons enter personnel at the clerical level and attend college part time. Some companies have in-service training programs to teach beginning personnel workers the operations and personnel procedures.

Specialized training or advanced degrees may be required for some jobs. This is understandable in light of the increasing complexity of employee benefit programs, government regulations, wage agreements, and employee selection procedures. The growing emphasis on professionalization in the field, resulting from increased specialization, has encouraged human resources management staff members to continue their educational growth throughout their working careers. Many personnel/human resources managers now hold master's degrees.

REQUIREMENTS FOR EMPLOYMENT

Educational preparation is necessary to enable personnel to perform the duties required of them. Preparation needed for entry and service at the various levels is described below.

For Entry at the Clerical Level

A high school diploma will usually be required for entry into the career field of personnel/human resources at the clerical level. In high school your course work should include English, mathematics, and a general foundation in science, followed by courses to prepare you for office work, such as typing, shorthand, letter writing, office procedures, office machines, calculators, computers, and other related skill courses. To be a successful personnel worker at the clerical level, you will utilize all of these skills in the performance of your duties.

For Service at the Specialist Level

At the specialist level you will be building on the skills acquired at the clerical level. The same skills will be used, but they will have to be developed to a much higher degree. Special schooling, such as shorthand, Stenomask, Dictaphone, or bookkeeping may be required. At this level you as a personnel worker may expand into payroll or payroll accounting or related duties. It is frequently convenient to have a specialist in the personnel office qualified as a notary public. Service at the specialist level requires highly polished office and secretarial skills, including computer operation.

For Entry at the Technical Level

A college degree is almost universally required for entry into the career field of personnel/human resources at the technical level. This is the level of first-line management. At this level the particular functions are managed and supervised. As a manager at this level you will be most valuable if you have a good, rounded education in the arts and sciences as well as a foundation in business and a broad understanding of personnel management. Furthermore, you will need an in-depth appreciation of one or more of the technical functions of personnel. At this level of the organization, you will use your technical knowledge of personnel to develop programs in your areas of technical specialty and to supervise the performance of these particular functions. You will be most valuable when you have a detailed knowledge and practical understanding of your particular functional areas. You will have to manage the function and provide leadership for those under your jurisdiction.

For Service at the Managerial and Executive Levels

Persons serving at the managerial and executive levels of organizations will need a thorough knowledge of personnel/human resources in particular and a good understanding of business administration or public administration in general. Graduate education will usually provide the basis for an understanding of the processes that the managers and executives will have to know to direct satisfactorily. Many managers and executives who do not have graduate degrees, master's and doctorates, have acquired the necessary knowledge through a vast amount of reading and experience. At these higher levels of management, there is a limit to the amount you as a manager will learn from formal education. After acquiring a particular knowledge of personnel/human resources, a general knowledge of business and public administration, and exposure to management development processes, it then is pretty much up to you how you will perform. At this stage, formal preparation has done as much as it can do. Now success becomes a matter of experience and your own initiative.

EDUCATIONAL PREPARATION

Preparation

Many employers seek to fill beginning positions in personnel and labor relations with college graduates who have the potential to move into management jobs. Some employers look for graduates who have majored in personnel/human resources management, while others prefer college graduates with a general business background. Still other employers feel that a well-rounded liberal arts education is the best preparation for personnel work. A college major in personnel administration, political science, or public administration can be an asset in looking for a job with a government agency.

At least 200 colleges and universities have programs leading to a degree in the field of human resources management. While personnel administration is widely taught, the number of programs that focus primarily on labor relations is quite small. In addition, many schools offer course work in closely related fields. An interdisciplinary background is appropriate for work in this area, and a combination of courses in the social sciences, behavioral sciences, business, and economics is useful.

Prospective personnel workers might apply courses in personnel management, business administration, public administration, psychology, sociology, political science, economics, and statistics. Courses in labor law, collective bargaining, labor economics, labor history, and industrial psychology provide a valuable background for the prospective labor relations worker.

Graduate study in human resources, economics, business, or law provides sound preparation for work in labor relations. While a law degree seldom is required for jobs at the entry level, many of the people with responsibility for contract negotiations are lawyers, and the labor-relations-plus-law-degree combination is becoming highly desirable.

A college education is important, but it is not the only way to enter personnel work. Some people enter the field at the clerical level and advance to professional positions on the basis of experience. They often find it helpful to take college courses part-time, however.

New personnel workers usually enter formal or on-the-job training programs to learn how to classify jobs, interview applicants, or administer employee benefits. After the training period, new workers are assigned to specific areas in the company's human resources department. After gaining experience, they usually can advance within their own company or transfer to another employer. At this point, some people move from personnel to labor relations work. Some people enter the labor relations field directly as trainees. They are usually graduates of MA programs in employee relations or law programs.

Workers in the middle ranks of a large organization often transfer to a top job in a smaller one. Employees with exceptional ability may be promoted to executive positions, such as director of personnel or director of labor relations.

Personnel/human resources workers should speak and write effectively and be able to work with people of all levels of education and experience. They also must be able to see both the employee's and the employer's point of view. In addition, they should be able to work as part of a team. They need supervisory abilities and must be able to accept responsibility. Integrity and fair-mindedness are important qualities for people in personnel/

human resources work. A persuasive, congenial personality can be a great asset.[19]

According to the Bureau of Labor Statistics, a bachelor's degree is the minimum educational background for a beginning job in personnel work, a field that includes such occupations as recruiter, interviewer, job analyst, position classifier, wage administrator, training specialist, and employee counselor. Some employers look for college graduates who have majored in personnel administration, public administration, business, or economics, while others prefer applicants with a liberal arts background and evident management potential. An analysis of the occupational field of personnel, training, and labor relations specialists and managers showed about 381,000 jobs in 1986. Significant growth is expected in the occupational field through the year 2000 at the rate of 1.4 percent per year.[20] Those interested in jobs in human resources management must be prepared to compete with the increasing number of applicants for human resources positions. Most openings will be occurring in smaller, newer firms in the private sector.

Cost of Education

An education is costly. Direct education costs might be considered to include tuition, fees, books, and supplies. Indirect costs include room and board, transportation, and personal expenses. Costs vary a great deal from one institution to another. However the following table reflects recent average costs.[21]

Transportation and personal expenses will vary widely and will depend on individual circumstances.

---

[19] *Occupational Outlook Handbook, 1988-89,* 39.

[20] Ibid.

[21] *College Cost Book: College Board Annual Survey of Colleges, 1988.* New York: College Entrance Examination Board.

Table 4-1. Education Costs

Item	*Four-year Private University*	*Four-year Public University*
Tuition and fees	$ 7,693	$1,566
Room and board	3,637	2,879
Books and supplies	427	411
Totals	$11,757	$4,856

Educational Opportunities

If you plan to go to college, the following references may be helpful:

ASPA Directory: A Directory of American Colleges and Universities (offering instruction in personnel and industrial relations)
American Society for Personnel Administration
606 North Washington Street
Alexandria, VA 22314

Lovejoy's Guide, 17th ed.
Published by Prentice-Hall Press, a division of Simon & Schuster
Gulf & Western Building
One Gulf & Western Plaza
New York, NY 10023

College Placement Annual
This is the official occupational directory of the Regional Placement Associations, providing information on the positions customarily offered to college graduates by principal employers. By contacting those firms in your geographical area, you could determine which ones, if any, are offering internships or other tuition benefits.

PROFESSIONAL CERTIFICATION

Almost all professional fields are making progress in the direction of requiring certification of their members. This serves two purposes: first, it ensures that members of the profession who hold the certification have met minimum professional standards of performance and meet the ethical standards of the profession. Second, it assures the public that those professionals who hold the appropriate designations are, in fact, qualified to perform the duties required of the profession.

For many years, accountants have had to pass stringent examinations to acquire the designation Certified Public Accountant (CPA). Medical doctors, after passing thorough examinations, are designated Doctors of Medicine (MD). Professionals in the field of personnel/human resources are now earning certification in the field through the Personnel Accreditation Institute (PAI). PAI is an independent, nonprofit, educational organization whose purpose is to raise and maintain standards in the personnel and human resources management field by:

- providing and updating periodically the outlines of the body of knowledge to accommodate growth and change in the field,
- promoting self-development of human resource professionals, and
- recognizing individual professionals who have mastered the defined body of knowledge.

Certification/accreditation is open to all professionals in the field—practitioners, educators, researchers, and consultants. It is given to specialists and to generalists based on their demonstrated mastery of the appropriate body of knowledge. Accreditation may be awarded at the basic or advanced level.

Functional Standards Committees for functional areas are responsible within the Institute for defining the body of knowledge, preparing study guides, and developing test questions. If you are interested in more information concerning accreditation, contact:

The Personnel Accreditation Institute
606 North Washington Street
Alexandria, VA 22314
703/548-3440

Most human resources people work in office settings. (California State University, Long Beach, photos)

CHAPTER 5

HOW TO GET STARTED

In any field, getting started is a tough proposition. There are many decisions to be made, and there are many unknowns that have to be investigated. Decisions are made at many points in a person's life, but those made from the age of about fifteen to about twenty-five may be the most important. During these years directions are taken that will have long-range effects on the careers of people. One's chances for success in life and in a chosen career are enhanced if the person will devote the time and effort necessary to analyze her or his position in life and consider the many things that must be done. The paragraphs that follow discuss the major aspects that one must consider in preparing and planning a career path. These things require time and mature contemplation.

SELF-EVALUATION

The first thing a person must decide is where he or she wants to be in life. Whatever the field or whatever the level, the person must decide where he or she wants to be in the distant future and express this desire in the broadest terms possible. "President of the XYZ Company" is too specific. "A top-level executive in manufacturing" is more general and better to start with.

Next, a person must analyze where he or she is. This should result in as complete a description as possible. For example, an adolescent might describe himself or herself as a seventeen-year-old high school junior, in Los Angeles, California.

After a person has decided where he or she wants to be and has analyzed where he or she is, he or she can take the next step and plan how to narrow the gap between the two. The route from being a high school junior to being a top executive would include a college degree, years of hard work, graduate study, and a wide variety of experiences. Realizing this early in life can facilitate planning the career path as one goes along. It is essential that a person keep in mind life objectives and career objectives so that one always knows the proper course to steer. With these things in mind, a person can make judgments whether certain activities will contribute to the attainment of those objectives or not.

This whole process, of course, is not simple. It involves many questions, and some of these will be discussed in the paragraphs that follow.

Objectives

Let's get down to the nuts and bolts of where you want to be. You must define as carefully as possible your life objectives and your career objectives. Life objectives might include such things as being extremely wealthy, working out of doors, or making a contribution to society. Career objectives might include such things as being a top-level accountant, being a research chemist, being a minister, or driving a bus. The immediate follow-up activity is to analyze where you are and then decide or plan how to get from where you are to where you want to be.

Resources

A careful analysis of your resources will help provide a realistic look at the range of possibilities for developing a career. Lack of resources should not deter you from striving for your stated objectives. A realistic appraisal of your resources will permit an honest understanding of the tools you can use to reach your objectives.

KINDS OF RESOURCES

Financial

It takes money to pay for an education. It takes money to pay for food and lodging. If your family is very hard pressed for money, then an overriding consideration regarding your future may be the necessity for you to get a job and support yourself or possibly even contribute to the support of the family group. If your family is in the middle income bracket, possibly there is enough to support you through your college education without the necessity for your getting a job. This could be complicated, however, if there are five students to be put through college one after another. Serious illness in the family will have an impact on the financial resources available to you in support of your efforts to get started in your education or your career.

Self-appraisal

Successful career planning demands an honest self-appraisal. This evaluation includes an estimate of your own intellectual capacity and motivation. Without motivation all the "smarts" in the world won't get you where you want to go. Without the intellectual capacity to meet the requirements of the career field, motivation is not enough. In borderline cases, the will and drive to succeed will help immensely, but it can overcome just so much. If you got D's and F's in school, there is little likelihood that you have the capacity to be a nuclear physicist. We have to face the fact that half of us have below average intelligence. This statement is a little severe, for most of us are very near the average. Some people are smarter than the average. Some are not as smart as the average. Most people are at or near the average. But those of us who are near the average must acknowledge that we are not above the average and therefore do not have the capacity to meet some extremely high and difficult requirements. There is a suitable job somewhere for each of us. Aiming for the impossible is only going to frustrate those of us who do not have the required intelligence and drive.

Education

With a realistic understanding of your objectives and the resources available, educational requirements and their attainment can be considered. Some career objectives will obviously require a college education, and some will require study at the graduate level. A business manager, for example, will have to have a bachelor's degree, and it is advisable for him or her to have a master of business administration (MBA) as well. This study generally takes about six years—four for the bachelor's and another two for the master's.

Will your resources stretch to meet this requirement? If not, then you will have to consider the alternatives. One is to take the lightest full-time study load possible and work during the summers and vacation breaks. In other words, you might go to school full-time and work part-time. Another alternative might be to go to school part-time and work full-time. You can get a better job this way, but it takes a much longer time to get the education required to reach your objectives. These are the realities of life, and the wise person will acknowledge that these problems exist and will face up to them and figure how to cope with them. Wishing will not make them go away. They must be faced and overcome.

JOB OR SCHOOL?

One of the decisions most of us have to face at some time is the choice between taking a job and going to school. If your financial resources are limited, there may not actually be the opportunity to make a choice—it may be made for you. Without money it may be necessary to get a full-time job to support yourself. In that case, the education takes second place, but it need not be set aside entirely. Many people work full-time and go to school part-time. This makes the process of getting an education longer, but it is possible and is chosen by many energetic, career-seeking people.

There are many advantages to going to school full-time. The most evident one is that the years spent in the educational process are reduced to the minimum. Another is that the job seeker has the best possible foundation before going out into the job market to find employment. Many students work part-time while going to school full-time.

There are, of course, many choices between studying full-time and working full-time. From one extreme to the other, they could be considered as full-time study with no work, full-time study with part-time work, half-time study with half-time work, part-time study with full-time work, and no study and full-time work. We all can learn more about our work, our environment, and our society. We should all strive to improve ourselves.

COUNSELING

We all need counseling occasionally. We need counseling in our work and in our choice of educational paths. No one should ever feel embarrassed to ask for assistance and counseling.

Counseling is the process of helping others evaluate things that concern them. Through the technique of discussion, the counselor can assist people to clarify their goals in life. A counselor can help someone make an honest appraisal of their own financial and family resources and needs. The most effective counselor doesn't advise anyone what to do. Rather, the effective counselor assists people to think things through for themselves. Good counselors are experienced in asking the right questions and probing for key information. When counselors probe people's private lives, they are not hunting for gossip. They are doing their job thoroughly by helping people take into consideration those aspects of their lives that they may have taken for granted. Matters such as the number of years a supporting parent has yet to work may have an effect on the financial resources available to put a young person through college. If the parent is sixty-five and will be forced into retirement at seventy, this is an important factor. Yet, most of us figure that our parents will go on forever.

The counselor will assist you to keep things in perspective. A high school or community college counselor is well equipped to outline the requirements and opportunities in a wide variety of careers. The counselor can explain in some detail the length of time required to complete the training or college required for career preparation, what the costs are likely to be, what the opportunities for landing a job might be, and how these things all relate to your resources, needs, and objectives.

No competent counselor will tell you what to do. No one should do that. You must make your own decisions. But the counselor can furnish information that will help you make decisions based on the most reliable data available. You have to live with the decisions you make, but the counselor can assist in relating requirements to resources.

Counseling is most effective when the student has done some homework first. For example, the student may be asked by the counselor, "What do you want to do?" If the student replies, "I don't know—that's what I came in here to find out," the student isn't prepared for an effective counseling session. The student has to have some idea of what kinds of things he or she likes to do and what her or his intellectual and financial resources are. The most effective counseling session results from the student doing as much preparation as possible prior to the session. Then the counselor can take the student from that point and help the student find the way better among the vast number of selections available in both educational choices and career paths.

At the high school level there are generally two kinds of counseling available: career counseling and college counseling. The first is intended to assist the student in finding a career field of interest. The second is intended to assist the student to find a college or university that offers the kinds of courses that will provide career preparation in a particular major field. College counseling can be in general terms, such as business administration, or more specific terms, such as personnel management.

At junior colleges and community colleges excellent counseling is usually available. One particular community college in California,[22] for example, is typical and offers extensive counseling in career information and college guidance services.

Career information services include educational and career information on job descriptions, placements, labor markets, licensing and certification, federal and state employment, military service opportunities, guides to careers through college majors, occupations, delivery systems, college and university catalog microfilm libraries, professional publications, industry news, college planning, university departmental bulletins and brochures, community college career programs, and others. This service also includes vocational testing and planning, career counseling, cooperative education services, and vocational planning classes.

College guidance services include counseling in particular academic divisions of the college. They also include career information services such as career counseling, career infor-

---

[22] Golden West College, Huntington Beach, California.

mation, guidance programs, and college and university catalogs.

The extent of the assistance available is illustrated by the outline of career planning services which include the following:

- Career information services for feeder high school students
- Career planning information and assistance
- Labor market and current job information
- Part-time job experiences for students
- Job performance upgrading
- Full-time job placement service for graduates and others discontinuing education
- Educational planning for career preparation
- On-campus employer recruitment

A catalog of career training programs is available. This catalog includes a description of all the career programs offered and provides a description of job duties and working conditions, job preparation, and the employment outlook and advancement.

Counseling is also available at four-year colleges and universities. Educational counseling and testing is usually available in the counseling office. Career counseling is usually available in the office dealing with career planning and placement. The titles of these offices vary from institution to institution, but the services will usually be provided somewhere on the campus.

Some counseling assistance and career information are often available from labor unions, professional organizations, and public service agencies. These would all have to be contacted individually for the services needed.

APPLYING FOR WORK

Eventually you must apply for work. With a high school diploma you can expect to be considered for a position at the clerical or beginner's level. With a bachelor's degree, you might expect to be considered for a position at the lower levels of management, assuming the degree major is related in some way to the requirements of the job being applied for. With a bachelor's degree and work experience, you might apply for a position at the middle management level. With a master's degree and experience, you could reasonably expect employment at the middle management level if your performance in previous assignments was generally excellent.

Whatever the level, there are certain procedures and mechanics you must go through to land a job. First, a job has to be located. This might result from scanning the want ads in the local newspaper, or a friend may advise you of an opportunity in her or his company. If you seem to have the qualifications to perform the job, then apply.

In order to apply for a position, you must file or complete an application form. This might be done by mail or in person in the personnel office or employment office of the company where the work is available. Each organization has its own particular application form. They are all a little different, but most of them will require the same kinds of information. The purpose of the application form is to inform the prospective employer of some of the basic information it must have concerning those who apply for work there.

Most application forms will contain spaces for the following information or questions:

- Name, address, phone number, Social Security number, and legality of residency status
- Position applied for: how did you learn of this opening?
- Age: are you over 18 and under 70?
- Statement of physical condition to perform the required work
- Statement of veteran status
- Education: level and name of each school attended, number of years attended, grade completed, special courses, diploma, degree

- Extracurricular activities
- Honors
- Employment history for last three jobs or last ten years (employer; address; immediate supervisor; your position, title, and duties; starting salary; reason for leaving.)

In addition to the application form, many organizations also utilize a confidential data sheet. This sheet is used to meet the requirements of the U.S. Department of Health and Human Services to compile summary data of the sex and ethnicity of applicants for positions. These sheets will typically contain information that may not appear on the application form and thus possibly constitute the basis for discrimination in hiring. The confidential data sheet is kept separate from the application form until after the successful applicant has been hired. After the person has won the job, the data sheet provides the statistical information that the employer is required to maintain and report.

A typical confidential data sheet would contain the following items of information:

- Name, address, phone number, Social Security number, and citizenship status
- Position applied for
- Sex, birthdate, physical condition

- Ethnic identification:

American Indian	Other Non-White
Black	White
Mexican/American	Filipino
Spanish surnamed	Do not choose to provide this information.
Asian American	

- How the applicant learned of the vacancy.

The Personnel/Human Resources Office

All personnel matters are administered in the personnel office of the organization. When you apply for work, you may be directed to file an application in the personnel office or sometimes, in very large firms, in the employment office established for this specific purpose. When you enter one of these offices, you will see an array of clerical and other office workers engaged in a variety of duties all related to personnel work.

There are several kinds of people you can expect to encounter in the personnel office.

Receptionist. This is the person who will greet you on entering the office and determine what assistance you need. You will, of course, need an application form and instructions necessary for completing it. The form might be filled out at a counter or in a room set aside for that purpose.

Interviewer. After completing the application form, you may expect to see an interviewer. The interviewer talks with you about the information on the application form to make sure that it is clear to you. The interviewer is able to explain many aspects of the position you are applying for. The general work rules of the organization may be described by the interviewer. One of the main purposes of the interview is to ensure that as an applicant you meet the requirements of the position and that you understand the requirements of the position and want the job.

Tester. After the interview is completed, it is possible that specified tests will be administered. For example, persons applying for secretarial jobs can expect to be given a typing test and possibly a shorthand test. Sometimes other tests are administered in the office or elsewhere in the place of work.

Others. There will be others in the personnel office who are engaged in various duties. Among those who might be observed are the records clerks who maintain the personnel files. The benefits clerk or counselor may be observed advising employees concerning the benefits of the retirement program. And that person rushing through the office with a harried look is probably the director of personnel.

Procedure

The usual hiring procedure will include those steps that have just been described—completing the application, the preliminary interview, and any required testing. When you pass all these hurdles, you will be referred to the prospective supervisor for the job interview. The supervisor is the person who will actually oversee the work of the new employee and thus is interested in the qualifications and experience of the applicant. The supervisor is also interested in those things that might be indicative of your success on the job. These would include your aptitudes, manner, sincerity, and response to the questions posed by the prospective supervisor. It is the supervisor who usually makes the decision to hire. The successful applicant will be informed and then will have to go through the hiring procedure, which entails getting more information and completing additional forms such as next of kin and beneficiary statements.

CHAPTER 6

HOW TO LAND THE JOB

MARKETING YOURSELF

Job hunting is a tough, competitive process. Few of us are handed a job on a silver platter. If the world hasn't beaten a path to your door by now, you may assume that you are going to have to go out into the cruel world and look for a job yourself. Most of us have to present ourselves to prospective employers and convince them that they should hire us. With this in mind, it might be wise to consider some questions that the employer could ask during an interview:

Why should I hire you?
What are your qualifications?
What experience have you had?
How have you prepared yourself for employment?
Why have you come to this particular organization for work?

One way or another these questions will have to be answered. In the paragraphs that follow, approaches to the answers are discussed. Keep one thing in mind. You will have to do all the work in connection with landing a job. It is a full-time undertaking. It's your livelihood, and you should consider it worthwhile to give the process the care and attention necessary to land the best job you can get.

THE RÉSUMÉ

People seeking employment at all levels of management and the top levels of white collar work should have a résumé prepared. The résumé is a brief outline of the applicant's qualifications and includes matters related to education, work experience, and other experiences that might point to the necessary qualifications to perform in the job.

There are many sources for information concerning the basic preparation of a résumé, so these will not be discussed at length here. The nearest counseling office will have handouts concerning the preparation of résumés. They are useful and should be consulted.

Keep in mind that the résumé is essentially a written communication from you to the prospective employer. It should tell important things about you clearly, and it should hold the interest of the reader. Just as a short story must hook the reader's interest and then hold it throughout the tale, the résumé must do the same. Therefore, the résumé should state your name, address, phone number, and then some statement of your objective. This tells the reader who you are and what you want. The arrangement of the remainder of the résumé is up to you. In general, however, if you wish to retain the reader's interest, you will have to set forth your qualifications and experience in the sequence that will be most likely to hold the reader's interest. If your education is strong, put that next. If not, put it towards the end. If your work experience is strong, put that near the top.

How do you decide what is important? That really is up to you since you are trying to market yourself to a prospective employer. Specific items and their relative importance follow.

Most Important Items

Your name, address, telephone number, the date you are available for employment, your job objective, education and honors, foreign languages you speak, military service or veteran status, history of past employment, community activities, memberships, and offices in professional associations are the items that provide useful and important information to prospective employers.

Least Important Items

The years you got your degrees, overall grade averages, awards and scholarships, grades in your college minor, your class standing, honorary societies, student body offices, and hobbies can be omitted. Personal data such as marital status, height, weight, number of children, spouse's occupation or education, parental information, or religious preference must not appear in order to avoid charges of discrimination in hiring.

These comments should be taken as guides rather than absolute rules. Not everyone experienced in the field of employment will agree with all of the opinions expressed. These rules do, however, provide a coordinated guide for preparing résumés.

THE TECHNIQUE

There are several ways of distributing your résumé to those who might be interested in hiring you. One system is simply to broadcast it to any and all organizations that might hire people with your qualifications in your area of interest. Return from this technique is very small, but coverage is very wide. With enough hooks in the water, you ought to catch a fish.

Another technique is to send out a one-page résumé covered with a one-page letter. This has the advantage of providing the most information in the smallest package for the employer to read. The letter should contain information that is not contained in the résumé. For example, the reader will wonder why you are writing. Reasons might include that you are just getting your college degree and are looking for a job. It might be that you have a job but are looking for one with more challenge and greater potential for promotion. Maybe you are changing from one career field to another. There are many legitimate reasons for job hunting. The reader will want to know yours. When using this technique, it is worth the trouble to go to the nearest library and use the current edition of *Standard and Poor's* or *Dun and Bradstreet* or some other industrial index to find the name and title of the top person in the organization you plan to address. If you are applying for a job in personnel, then you will want the name and correct title of the top person in human resources management. Address your letter to that person by name.

LOCATING THE OPPORTUNITIES

Job opportunities appear in a number of sources. The job seeker will have to pursue all the leads available in order to ensure the best coverage.

Although there are private agencies that help people find work for a fee, several free agencies are also available.

Public Services

All states have employment offices located in major cities and in central locations. Employment offices are interested in the qualifications of the job seeker and the kind of position he or she is looking for. The same offices also keep records of job opportunities listed by organizations. The employment offices try to match the job opportunities with the job applicants.

Advertising

Firms that have job openings also may advertise in the local newspapers or in professional publications and trade journals such as the *Wall Street Journal, The Personnel Administrator,* and the *Personnel Journal.* These publications are available at the local public library in most cities. They may also be available in school libraries. When looking for jobs, check the headings, "Personnel," "Labor Relations," "Human Resources Management," or any of the occupational areas of your particular interest.

When looking for employment, comb through the want ads in the local newspaper. These ads should be checked carefully to determine if you have the qualifications listed in the ad. If not, it may well be fruitless to respond. If you're close, it might be worth a try, but don't expect too much.

When responding to an ad be sure to respond to each point made in the ad. This can be done in the letter covering the résumé. This action simply serves to emphasize that you have the qualifications the company has deemed important enough to specify in the ad.

If the employer is named in the ad, you may want to consider whether you want to work for that company. If the employer is not identified—that is, you are asked to respond to a box number—you are responding blindly. Some firms place ads this way to avoid offending present employees or having to answer all applications. Responding to an ad should be done just as carefully as sending out résumés and cover letters.

Placement Offices

Most colleges and universities have placement offices that assist job-seeking students. They usually act as centers where students can arrange placement interviews with various company representatives.

Counseling Offices

Many high schools have career counseling offices in addition to college counseling offices. Young people interested in careers in professional fields, such as personnel/human resources, should check in both offices for information concerning job openings and career preparation.

Undecided?

Maybe you're not sure that you'd really enjoy a particular kind of career. Is it possible to get an idea during high school? Yes—volunteering to help in the counseling office during free periods or after school will help you decide whether you like working with people. Volunteering to cover an information desk is also good experience. Visiting personnel departments in local businesses and industries and observing personnel workers on their jobs are perhaps the best ways to judge your interest in that field.

THE JOB INTERVIEW

The job interview provides the opportunity for the applicant and the management of the firm to become acquainted with each other. Even though the employer has already read your résumé and your application, there are many more things he or she wants to know about you. If you and all other applicants are equally well qualified for the position you are applying for, the only differences between the candidates are those that will show up in the interview. It behooves the applicants to prepare for the interview and to present themselves at their best.

Preparation

Do your homework. Know something about the firm and the key people you may see. This can be done by looking up the company in the latest edition of *Dun and Bradstreet* or *Standard and Poor's* compilations of information on American businesses. This knowledge will strengthen your background for discussions in the job interview. An outline of information and points you wish to make or find out about is very helpful.

Groom yourself properly. This means clean clothes and a neat and fresh appearance. The company is less interested in the details of your dress and grooming, such as beard or length of hair, but it will expect you to be suitably dressed for a management position, wearing clothes of contemporary style but not so extreme as to be distracting. Dress and grooming should be appropriate for the place of employment, kind of work, and your age.

Techniques

The interview is a give-and-take procedure. When you are asked a question, answer it thoroughly but briefly. It takes practice and judgment to determine when a question has been answered completely. But it is important not to go too far. If a brief answer is not enough, the interviewer will ask for more details. You will make a good impression on the interviewer if you help by giving the information he or she seeks. Few managers know how to interview well. Help the interviewer get the information he or she wants.

You will have some control over the direction and depth of the interview. Tell the interviewer about yourself, but try to hold something back. If the interviewer wants to know more, he or she will say so.

Try for a win in each interview. Be enthusiastic and know

what you are talking about. Don't carry a briefcase or résumés with you into the interview room. Take notes and paper in your pockets. It helps to be articulate and to use correct English.

What to Say

In your comments, mention your interest in that particular firm. Demonstrate that you already have some knowledge of the industry, its processes, and developments. Mention your qualifications in general terms. You might highlight interesting aspects of your studies, work experiences, or travel. There will be an opportunity for you to mention what you believe you can contribute to the firm. This might be youth, imagination, or vigor. You must believe that you have something going for you. Go ahead and mention it. Don't brag, but learn how to put yourself forward in a factual way. Mention specific accomplishments without boasting of what great things they were. You state the facts. Let others judge the degree or quality of the achievement.

You will usually be given the opportunity to ask questions or state particular interests. You should be able to do two things: first, be prepared to make a statement of personal objectives that will be consistent with the objectives of the firm. Second, don't ever let the opportunity go by without expressing an interest in more knowledge about the firm. For example, always be ready to say, "I'd like to know more about...."

What to Do

Do your best. Try hard to make a good impression. Put your best foot forward. Your manner should be pleasant, interested, and it should reflect relaxed self-control.

Try to get the interviewer to talk about the position, the company, the industry, how long he or she has been with the firm, and what the greatest current problem is. Find out why the position you are applying for is open. If it is a new position, that is one thing. If the last employee in the position got fired, watch out—someone may be waiting in the shadows to do the same to you. If, however, that employee got promoted, that is quite another thing. Listen carefully for key facts and attitudes. Probe these matters very carefully. This phase of the interview gives you the opportunity to learn more about the firm and, particularly, about the position you have applied for. If the interviewer answers your questions in a straightforward manner, then you can learn much about what you may be facing. If the interviewer is evasive, be careful, it may be difficult to pinpoint what is wrong, but you can bet that something is awry if the interviewer will not answer questions candidly.

What Not to Do

Avoid telephone interviews. These put you at an unnecessary disadvantage. You'll do better face to face. If a firm is really interested in you, it will extend you the courtesy of an interview in person.

Avoid jokes and strained pleasantries. They can easily bomb on you. Easy pleasantries are all right. Avoid arguments. Rather than argue, probe the bases of the opinions held by others. You will learn more from this and also exhibit an interest in the views of the other person.

Never give references without checking first to get their approval. Don't name your references until you and your prospective employer both seem to be favorably disposed toward your employment in that organization. Get the best references you can. Avoid any that you are not sure will be favorable.

Salary

Inquire about salary and fringe benefits only after all other major matters have been discussed. If the interviewer asks you what your salary requirements are, say that you cannot estimate your requirements until you have more information concerning the responsibilities and requirements of the position. You should go into the interview with a salary range in mind. A higher figure might be appropriate for greater responsibility and few fringes. A lower one might serve for lesser responsibility and many fringes. A pleasant work environment might serve to compensate for a somewhat lesser salary. Proximity to your home may be a factor.

Eventually, you will have to ask what is being offered, or the interviewer will have to know your requirements. This is the time for some plain talk and maybe some negotiations. You should be aware of the value of what you have to offer a prospective employer. You can find some information concerning going wages in the latest wage survey of your geographical area and occupational field published by the U.S. Department of Labor, Bureau of Labor Statistics.

Follow-up Contact

After the interview and within two days, write a letter to the person who interviewed you. Do not write a trite or flowery letter of thanks for the interview. Instead, review the highlights of the interview. Bring up any additional pertinent points, especially any that might help the interviewer solve problems raised in the interview. Add any strengths or experiences that may not have been covered in the interview for lack of time. Don't get petulant. Just inquire about the status of your application for the position and express your continued interest in it.

Self-development

Each interview should be used as a learning experience. The interview should be analyzed by you in order to learn what to do and what not to do. Each interview presents the opportunity for self-development as a result of a careful analysis of the good and bad aspects of the interview.

Note the highlights of the interview. Make a record of names, addresses, titles, phone numbers, and relationships of those who interviewed you or those whose names came up during the interview. Critique the interview in terms of strengths and weaknesses. Be sure to take any follow-up action indicated, such as contacting someone; or looking up some statistics or the provisions of a particular act of legislation.

If an interview doesn't result in a job offer, don't get discouraged. You will be fortunate if out of every one hundred contacts you make you get five job interviews, and from those, one job offer.

If you had ninety-nine unproductive interviews, don't let it get you down. You should approach that one hundredth interview with just as much enthusiasm as you approached the first and with a lot better preparation. You should do better—after all, think of all the experience you've had now. Hang in there and keep trying!

Computers are playing an increasingly important role in the human resources workplace. (IBM photo)

CHAPTER 7

GETTING AHEAD

Many first jobs are part-time work with which students pay part of their school or living expenses. If you can find a part-time job while still in school, you will be one step ahead.

Your first employment in a personnel career could very well be a job as a junior interviewer, personnel clerk, assistant job analyst, or labor relations assistant, depending on your education, experience, and the position available. After getting some work experience, and sometimes, in-service training, you may move up to become the head of a department and eventually go to a top personnel/human resources position. Some personnel executives who reach the top of their department in a small company transfer to a larger firm with more sophisticated personnel programs and higher salaries. As the labor force expands and as the demand on personnel departments broadens, it becomes increasingly possible for personnel managers to become top-level managers of their companies.

SUCCESS ON THE JOB

Success on the job will depend on three basic and essential aspects of all positions: knowledge of job content, performance on the job, and relationships on the job. *Job content* refers to knowing what is expected of you on the job and what things you are expected to know. This includes not only facts (what), but also the processes involved (how). These things relate to the rules and regulations, including legislation, that place certain requirements on the office. The requirements of the job will usually be contained in the job description. There may also be a position description that will provide more specific details of the content of the assignment. The employee in a position should be thoroughly familiar with these.

Performance on the job refers to the way you carry out your assignment. The speed and accuracy with which you do the tasks that constitute your job reflect on your total job performance. Managers usually look for thoroughness, accuracy, and speed in the duties of the assignment. This usually means that the person performing the job sets high standards of performance. To do your best in the job is to put forth a conscientious effort to give all that you are being paid for and more. If you are going to worry about doing more than you think you are getting paid for, you are hampering yourself. You will neither enjoy the assignment nor perform it well.

Few jobs are performed in isolation. Almost all assignments, and certainly all those in the field of personnel/human resources, require relationships with others at work. These others are your superiors, your colleagues, and those in other offices in the organization, as well as those outside the organization who have business dealings with your office and your position. In these relationships you must be able to understand work assignments given you and then carry out the tasks necessary to complete the assignment. You will be working in conjunction with the other workers in the same office and many others in other offices in the organization. These relations usually comprise the exchanging of information or the processing of papers in some sequential order such that the work one person does depends on the proper completion of the previous step. Relations external to the place of work will usually require the getting or giving of information. The successful worker will know how to communicate under these various circumstances.

ADVANCEMENT

Advancement in the organization will depend first on the existence of a vacancy or a need in the organization. Assuming there is such a vacancy in the organization, what can one do to get advanced?

Advancement may depend on two factors related to the persons themselves. First is the matter of how well they have performed in previous work assignments. Superior performance in the current or previous assignment is usually taken as an indicator of competence in that kind of assignment, and the inference is that the person will probably work equally well in a higher position.

Another key factor of consideration is preparation for the advanced assignment. Keep in mind that within any occupational field the differences at various levels within the field are represented by different degrees of skill and different degrees of responsibility. At the higher levels, the skills and responsibility are greater. The person seeking advancement to the higher level should be prepared to perform at the higher level of skill as well as to accept the higher level of responsibility.

It is not out of line to inform your superior that you seek work at a higher level in the organization. The supervisor will ask if you are prepared to perform at a higher level of skill and accept the greater responsibility. You could then demonstrate your higher level skills and assure the supervisor that you seek more responsibility. If you are not qualified, then you should ask the supervisor what preparation you need to qualify yourself for advancement. This shows the supervisor that you are interested and that you want to know what you must do to better prepare yourself for advancement. A good supervisor will always help subordinates prepare themselves for higher-level assignments, even though it means that eventually you will be leaving for another assignment and a replacement will have to be trained. In notifying your boss that you seek advancement, don't give her or him the impression that you are looking for a way out. Tell your supervisor how much you have learned from her or him, that you want to learn more, and also that you hope to qualify yourself for advancement.

In a profession such as personnel/human resources, it is usually assumed that beginners in the field will continue their education and development both on and off the job. Advancement depends on competent performance and development.

CHAPTER 8

THE OPPORTUNITIES

The anticipated increase in the nation's labor force is expected to create a need for more personnel workers to carry on existing activities and to handle new personnel problems as they arise. The outlook for personnel work is excellent, according to both industrial and government sources. Figure 8-1 shows the expanding work force and also the rapidly increasing number of workers employed in the field of personnel/human resources. The number of personnel workers is expected to increase into the 1990s as employers recognize the need to maintain good employee relations.

Although the competition is increasing, there are numerous openings for young people willing to start in subprofessional or junior level positions. A growing number of industrial and government employers are setting up in-service training programs for this purpose. Employment prospects will probably be best for college graduates who have specialized training in personnel/human resources management.

Employment in some specialized areas of personnel will rise faster than others. The need for labor relations experts to handle relations with unions will probably continue to increase. Growth of employee services, safety programs, training, personnel research, and pension and other benefit plans is also likely to continue. People trained in psychological testing and in handling work-related problems may find particularly good job prospects.

WHERE THE JOBS ARE

As of 1986, there were about 381,000 people working in the personnel field in virtually every industry. Specialists accounted for about 230,000 positions, the rest being managers. About 10,000—most of them specialists—were self-employed.

More than eighty-five percent of the salaried jobs were in the private sector. The largest employer, labor unions, accounted for eleven percent of all salaried jobs. Other major employers include management, consulting, public relations firms, educational institutions, hospitals, banks, temporary help agencies, and department stores.

Approximately fifteen percent of salaried human resources specialists and managers worked for federal, state, and local governments in 1986. They handled recruitment, interviewing, job classification, training, salary administration, employee relations, mediation, and related matters for the nation's seventeen million public employees: police officers, firefighters, sanitation workers, teachers, hospital workers, and others.[23]

Women

There is a continuing demand for women in industry. There will not only be more women employed, but more opportunities at higher levels of management. Capable women executives have been promoted to directors of personnel in many companies.

---

[23]*Occupational Outlook Handbook, 1988-89*, 39.

Minorities

Minority personnel are being sought by many companies to fill openings in the fields of personnel and labor relations. Persons with experience or specialized training are in even greater demand.

OUTLOOK

Most growth in the number of personnel/human resources specialists and managers will occur in the private sector as employers try to provide effective human resources programs for an expanding work force. Rapid employment growth is expected in management and consulting, as well as personnel supply firms (temporary help firms), as businesses increasingly contract out personnel functions or hire personnel specialists on a contractual basis. This is done to meet the increasing cost and complexity of training and development programs. Fast growth is also expected in health care, residential care, and related industries to accommodate the needs of a rapidly growing elderly population. Relatively little growth is anticipated in public personnel administration.[24]

Demand for human resources specialists and managers is governed by the staffing needs of the firms where they work. A rapidly expanding business is likely to hire additional personnel workers—either as permanent employees or consultants—while a business that is reducing its operations will require fewer personnel workers. In any particular firm, the size and the job duties of the human resources staff are determined by a variety of factors, including the firm's organizational philosophy and goals, the labor intensity and skill profile of the industry, the pace of technological change, government regulations, collective bargaining agreements, standards of professional practice, and labor market conditions.[25]

---

[24] *Occupational Outlook Handbook, 1988-89*, 40.

[25] Ibid.

There are additional factors that stimulate demand for personnel/human resources management specialists and managers. Legislation that set standards in occupational safety and health, equal employment opportunity, and benefits has substantially increased the amount of recordkeeping, analysis and report writing in the human resources management area. Data gathering and analytical activities will increase as employers continue to review and evaluate their personnel policies and programs. But that may not generate many additional jobs because of offsetting productivity gains associated with the automation of personnel and payroll information.[26]

---

[26] Ibid.

Table 8-1. Percent of Full-Time Employees Participating in Employee Benefit Plans, Private Industry, United States; 1986[a]

Employee Benefit Program	All Employees	Professional and Administrative Employees	Technical and Clerical Employees	Production Employees
Paid:				
Holidays	99	99	100	98
Vacations	100	99	100	100
Rest time	72	58	69	82
Sick leave	70	93	93	45
Personal leave	25	33	35	15
Lunch time	10	3	4	17
Accident and sickness insurance	49	28	35	69
Noncontributory[b]	41	22	28	59
Long-term disability insurance	48	68	60	30
Noncontributory[b]	38	52	47	24
Health insurance	95	96	94	96
Noncontributory[b]	54	52	45	61
Pension plan (defined benefit)	76	78	78	74
Noncontributory[b]	71	73	74	69
Life insurance	96	97	96	95
Noncontributory[b]	87	87	87	86

Source: U.S. Bureau of Labor Statistics, *Employee Benefits in Medium and Large Firms, 1985 and 1986*, Bulletins 2262 and 2281.
[a] Excluding Alaska and Hawaii.
[b] Provided at no cost to employee.

Figure 8-1 Work Force and Personnel Workers

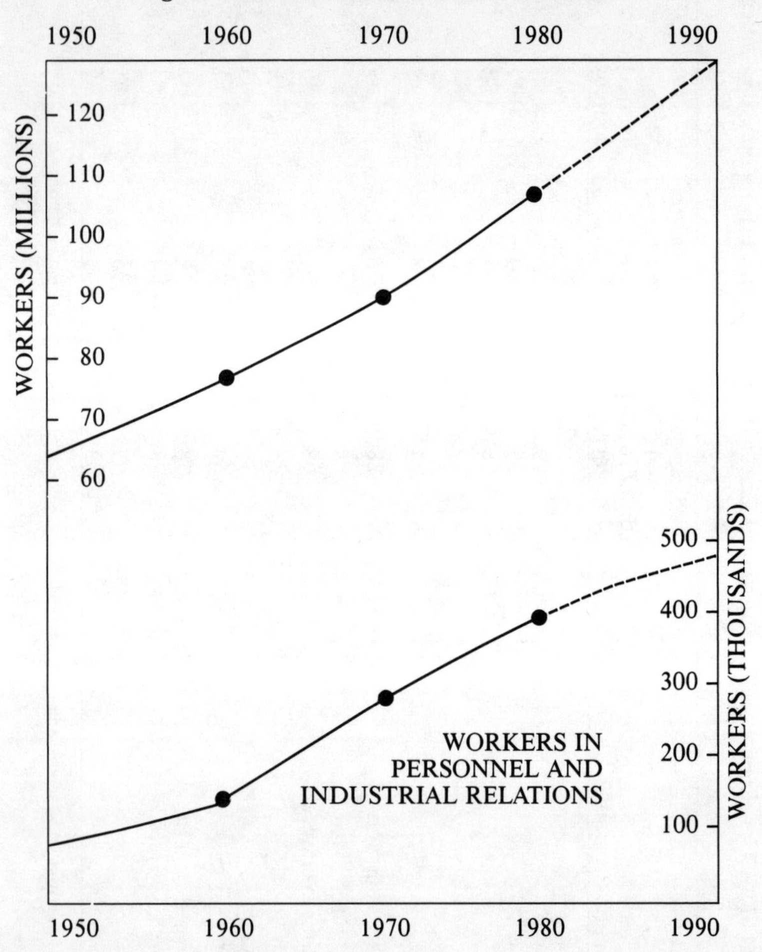

Source: Occupational Outlook Handbook, 1982-83 (Washington, D.C.: U.S. Department of Labor, Bureau of Labor Statistics, Bulletin 2200, 1982) and *Occupation Employment Matrix, 1970, 1978, and projected 1990. April 1981* (Washington: U.S. Department of Labor.)

CHAPTER 9

CURRENT ISSUES IN HUMAN RESOURCES MANAGEMENT

There are many current issues involving people at work that will have a major impact on human resources management. As a general rule, issues such as these take many years to resolve. Nevertheless, they are current and will have a major effect on the duties and functions performed in all departments of human resources management. Job seekers who tend to be indifferent about a career in human resources management might begin to think otherwise if they would consider some of the current issues in the field. These issues are not necessarily new, but they are in the forefront of social and business concerns today. Personnel/human resources workers are very involved in these issues, yet they do not constitute separate functions of personnel management as such. They are a major and continuing aspect of the total human resources program of any organization of substantial size. Some of the more important issues are discussed below.

CHILD CARE

The subject of child care refers to the care of preschool age children at the place of work. Why should companies offer child care options to their employees? The general response to that question involves the opinion that it is good business to do so. The number of women in the work force continues to increase. Currently forty-five percent of the work force is comprised of women and sixty percent of all children have mothers in the work force. We can expect that whatever child care program a company adopts, it will be administered in the department of human resources.

While many companies presently offer child care facilities, many others are studying the issue to determine the best approach for them. In general, these companies seek more employer information about child care programs and greater knowledge about employees' child care needs. There are tax advantages for employees choosing child care through a flexible benefits/savings plan. Companies require more information on the costs of providing child care. They perceive cost as one of the biggest obstacles to becoming more involved in child care programs. Regardless of company size, most companies consider they do not have a current assessment of their child care needs.

There are several approaches that companies can take to assist employees with their child care needs. The major ones are described briefly below.[27]

Financial Assistance. Direct financial assistance can be provided in several ways. The employer can offer a voucher system of allocating pre-tax dollars for child care or a flexible spending account through a flexible benefits program. Providing financial assistance supports the concept of parental choice in select-

---

[27] Derived from various sources from the American Society for Personnel Administration, Alexandria, Virginia.

ing their own child care, and it also helps parents meet rising child care costs.

Information Services. In providing these services, companies gather and disseminate information on child care available in the community. They may also provide counseling services that help working parents cope with family-related stress.

Company Owned/Sponsored Services. Activities such as employer-sponsored child care centers, centers provided by contractors, and child care consortiums are found in some companies. The consideration and provision of a child care center directly relates to company size. About half of the larger companies (more than 1500 employees) have at least explored the possibility of an employer owned/sponsored center. Although the most costly option, an advantage of an on-site center is that parents and children would stay closer together. Employees would spend less time in transportation to child care facilities, and tardiness to work would be reduced. A consortium (two or more companies splitting the cost of the child care center) has similar advantages. This choice works well for smaller companies.

Alternate Work Schedules. Work policies that may help accommodate parental needs include flextime, part-time work options, job sharing, work-at-home programs, and special summer or holiday hours. Employers appear to favor alternative schedules, especially part-time work, and flextime to assist with employees' child care needs.

Family Leave Options. There are several leave options presently used. First is pregnancy disability leave, either paid, unpaid, or partially paid. There is also maternity leave, also paid or unpaid and with other options. Additionally, there is paternity leave with paid, unpaid, and other options that are available. The type of leave offered most frequently is the pregnancy disability leave with pay. This is leave granted for pregnancy that ends after the woman gives birth and the doctor allows her to return to work. If the company has a disability policy, then, by law, it must include pregnancy as a disability. Maternity leave is defined as leave given the mother to be with her child, even though she is healthy and able to work. Almost all companies presently offer paid pregnancy disability leave for longer than four weeks. Companies have various combinations of paid and unpaid leave for differing lengths of time.

Although many problems relating to child care have been solved, there are other major issues to be dealt with. These include cost and liability, concern over equity of employee benefits, employer's familiarity with child care options, commitment from top management, and company involvement in family matters. Congress has been struggling with a wide variety of bills dealing with child care, but at the present no clear trend or intention is evident.

PARENTAL LEAVE

This is an issue that is closely related to child care. At issue here is whether parents should be granted leaves of absence from work to care for new or seriously ill children. Federal legislation dealing with this issue is currently under consideration. One bill requires that companies with more than twenty employees offer parental leave and guarantee an employee's job will be waiting upon completion of that leave. Another bill allows up to thirteen weeks of unpaid medical leave for workers who have been employed for at least one year. Additionally, workers would be entitled to up to ten weeks of unpaid leave to care for a newborn, adopted, or seriously ill child.

The legislation is designed to help American workers deal with crisis family situations without risk of losing their jobs. It is based on the philosophy that strong American families mean a stable and productive work force. Opponents of this legislation emphasize the enormous costs to the employers—possibly $500 million per year. They point out the necessity to hire temporary substitutes for employees on leave, loss of productivity, the loss of quality service in the service professions, and other severe impositions on management.[28]

MINIMUM WAGE

The current federally mandated minimum wage is $3.35 per hour. In accordance with the provisions of the Fair Labor Standards Act (FLSA), all persons covered by the law must be paid a minimum of $3.35 per hour. This rate came into effect in 1981 as a result of amendments to the Act made in 1977. Arguments in favor of increasing the minimum wage are based on the requirement for higher wages to meet increasing costs of living. Arguments against increasing the minimum wage include the adverse affect of higher wages on potential job opportunities for the very groups the higher wage is supposed to assist—that is, those at the lower end of the wage scale and new workers in the work place. Also minimum wage increases historically have tended to be inflationary. The 100th Congress, 1987-88, considered various bills proposing an increase in the minimum wage. None were passed. There is little doubt, however, that there will be continuing attempts to increase the minimum wage. It seems probable that in the near future a new minimum wage somewhere between $4.50 and $5.00 will become law.

WRONGFUL TERMINATION

The term *termination*, as we use it here, means discharge or total separation from the place of work. Wrongful termination means an act on the part of the employer that is illegal or an unfair labor practice. Some examples of wrongful termination

---

[28] Faze, James, "Parental leave measure reintroduced in Senate," in *Resource*, July 1988, monthly news on Human Resources Management, published by the American Society for Personnel Management, Alexandria, Virginia.

include discharging an employee for union organizing activities (an unfair labor practice), or terminating an employee because of age (illegal), or discharging an employee for "blowing the whistle" on an employer (without just cause). Several principles involved in discharge or termination warrant consideration.

Right to Manage. In order to operate, management must have the right to manage. That means to decide the business it is in, the assignment of work, the hiring and firing of employees, and many other aspects. It is an established maxim that management must have the right to take corrective action. That can mean reassignment, training, or disciplinary action, including discharge.

Job-as-property Doctrine. Many individuals believe that a job should be the property right of an employee. Because the loss of one's employment has such serious consequences, employees should not lose their jobs without the protection of due process as covered by the Fourteenth Amendment to the Constitution. This Amendment states, "Nor shall any state deprive any person of life, liberty, or property, without due process of law." Although the job-as-property doctrine does not guarantee employees a permanent right to their jobs, it does place upon management an obligation to act in a fair, consistent, and equitable manner toward its employees.[29]

Just Cause. In contemporary America, especially in those organizations that have agreements with labor unions, management's right to take corrective action must be based on just cause. This means that corrective action taken must be for clear, compelling, and justifiable reasons.[30] This suggests that management must build an airtight case against an employee it plans to take disciplinary action against, including discharge.

---

[29] Sherman, Bohlander, and Chruden, *Managing Human Resources*, 442.

[30] Ibid.

Employment-at-will. The employment relationship between a company and its individual employees has traditionally followed the common law doctrine of employment-at-will. This principle assumes that an employee has a right to sever the employment relationship for a better job opportunity or for other personal reasons. Employers, likewise, are free to terminate the employment relationship at any time—and without notice—for any reason, no reason, or even a bad reason. The employment-at-will relationship is created when an employee agrees to work for an employer for an unspecified period. Since employment is for an indefinite duration, it can be terminated at the whim of either party. In 1908 the Supreme Court upheld the employment-at-will doctrine.[31] There is clear evidence of contemporary trends in legal decisions to erode management rights under the employment-at-will doctrine. It may be a few years yet before the doctrine stabilizes.

RISK NOTIFICATION

In these days of environmental awareness, people at work are becoming more and more concerned about the hazardous materials used at the work place. Risk notification deals with the issue of management being required to inform employees of conditions and substances that have or might constitute an occupational hazard. Proposed legislation in the 100th Congress would have established a new bureaucracy within the Department of Health and Human Services that would notify current and former workers who had been exposed as many as thirty years ago to substances that now appear to present health risks. Any workers who received such a notification would be entitled to free medical monitoring, at employer expense, to determine if they are suffering from disease. All notified workers, regardless of whether they demonstrate any actual symptoms or illnesses, would be entitled to medical monitoring. Tests for chronic illnesses such as cancer and heart disease are seldom

[31] Ibid.

simple or inexpensive. These costs would in all likelihood be borne directly by the employer, since few health plans today would cover these unanticipated expenses.

At issue here is the obligation of management to provide a safe and healthful environment in which to work. Additionally, it involves the requirement to notify employees of past risks that may affect them now. Most human resources management professionals believe that employees should be informed of risks posed by hazardous substances they may be exposed to on the job. They oppose, however, measures that impose costly liability on all employers. Employers must already comply with OSHA regulations, which require telling employees of hazardous substances they may be exposed to on the job, as well as provide training on the safe handling of such substances. The costs of liability insurance, workers compensation, medical monitoring, and some reassignment rights under proposed legislation would be exorbitant.

Most of us are aware of the current attempts to remove asbestos from areas where people may be exposed to it, such as places of work and schools. Asbestos was installed for insulation before it was recognized as a cause of lung cancer. Now that its effects have been identified, it is being removed.

As we become more aware of the dangerous materials unknowingly installed in the past, we consider some measure necessary to identify affected workers and provide some corrective action. Such measures should encourage greater care in the use of new substances and provide some kind of remedial action for those who have been affected in the past. Measures that would have catastrophic financial effect on organizations will not serve the interests of the public in the long run. We can anticipate some legislation dealing with risk notification, and the required programs that are sure to be administered under the jurisdiction of an organization's department of human resources.

HEALTH CARE INSURANCE

Health care insurance is hotly contested today. Costs are rising sharply and have done so for some years. Benefits in the past included medical, surgical, and hospital expenses. Today, employers are under great pressure to include prescription drugs, eye care, dental care, and mental health care. Most organizations today provide some type of group medical insurance for their employees and their dependents. Skyrocketing medical costs have resulted from federal legislation, increased cost of retiree benefits, changes in Medicare pricing, the aging work force, and technological advances in medical practice that resulted in higher costs rather than financial savings. Attempts to contain costs include mandatory second surgical opinions, increased coordination of benefits, higher deductibles, and incentives for outpatient surgery and testing.[32]

Legislation was introduced in the last Congress that would mandate all employers, regardless of size, to provide a minimum level of health insurance to all employees and their dependents. The bill would have required an employer to provide a plan that would:

- cover all medically necessary hospital care, physician care, diagnostic tests, and prenatal and well-baby care;
- provide catastrophic protection against serious illness, with a cut-off of $3000 in out-of-pocket expenses;
- limit deductibles to $250 a person and $500 a family, and copayments from employees to twenty percent of the cost of any service.

The bill would have required employers to pay eighty percent of the cost of health care premiums.

---

[32] Sherman, Bohlander, and Chruden, *Managing Human Resources*, 556.

Most of us favor some measure to protect workers against catastrophic illnesses. That is, we don't want to see persons unprotected against the unavoidable costs of illnesses that cause a worker a personal/financial catastrophy. No one benefits from this. It seems only reasonable, however, that there be some limit to the obligation of the employer or the general public to provide protection to the others. Most human resources management professionals oppose the federal government imposing mandated benefits on the private sector employer. To restrict the flexibility of an employer to shape a benefit plan tends to work against the employees themselves. Employees know what kind of benefits they want. Imposing uniformity and mandating benefit plans that have traditionally been mutually determined by workers and employers, is not consistent with the basic concept of free enterprise and interferes with the well-established principles of flexible benefits for employees. It seems certain that there will be federal legislation on this subject in the near future, and that resulting programs will be administered within the department of human resources.

AIDS AND THE WORK PLACE

Dealing with employees who have been diagnosed as victims of Acquired Immune Deficiency Syndrome (AIDS) is one of the most challenging issues in the field of human resources management today. One aspect of the issue is the nature of the illness itself, while another is the obligation of management to treat the afflicted person as handicapped or not.

When the general public first became aware of the existence of AIDS and its universally fatal nature, there was great feeling of repugnance and fear of incidental transmission of the disease or virus. Later we learned that the disease cannot be transmitted through incidental contact. There is general agreement now that AIDS is transmitted by blood, semen, and breast milk. The method of transmission is usually through blood transfusion, sexual contact, or contaminated hypodermic needles. With greater understanding of these matters, we can now calm down and consider the issue of what to do about persons in the work place who have AIDS. Some of the necessary decisions have been made for us by decisions of the courts. But the incidence of AIDS is increasing in America and throughout the world, and the directives dealing with contemporary conditions may not be adequate for future conditions. We can best prepare for future action if we know a little more about AIDS and management's role under present laws and interpretations.

Four stages of the AIDS disease have been identified. In stage one the employee appears healthy but is a carrier of the AIDS virus. This person may remain healthy for the duration of his or her life or could later develop overt AIDS and the HTLV III/LAV spectrum of diseases. In stage two the employee begins to show signs of AIDS Related Complex (ARC). At this time the person exhibits prolonged symptoms of fatigue, fevers, night sweats, weight loss, and persistent diarrhea. Physical deterioration of the employee can have a significant impact on work performance. During stage three the employee contracts an opportunistic infection—one which does not normally arise in a healthy individual. Pneumonia is the most common opportunistic infection found in stage three. Finally, in stage four the employee has multiple infections leading to total incapacity and then to death.[33]

Management has a very touchy role to enact in relation to employees who have AIDS. It must meet its obligation to operate the organization, to consider the health and welfare of all its employees, to be fair with those who are victims of AIDS, and manage within the provisions of applicable legislation. The Vocational Rehabilitation Act of 1973, a federal law, prohibits

---

[33] Franklin, Geralyn McClure and Robert K. Robinson, "AIDS and the Law," in *Personnel Administrator*, American Society for Personnel Administration, April 1988, 118-121.

discrimination against otherwise qualified handicapped individuals solely on the basis of their disability. The law, however, only protects persons who are able to perform the essential functions of the job in spite of the handicap. While the Justice Department has generally regarded AIDS as a handicap, it also holds that discharge because of fear of contagion is not discrimination on the basis of a handicap. Therefore, the department concludes that such discrimination is not illegal. A question then arises, "Under what circumstances does contagious disease remove a handicapped individual from full protection of the act?" When can an employer terminate a contagious employee and not be in violation of the act? Two further questions arise; one is the issue of "risk to others," and the other issue is "otherwise qualified."[34]

The question of "risk to others" depends upon the answers to four questions posed by the American Medical Association. The first concerns the nature of the risk and relates to how the disease is transmitted. The next question considers the duration of the risk or how long the carrier is infectious—once infected, the employee is contagious for life. Then there is the question of severity of potential risk to third parties. Lastly, there is the question of the probability that the disease will be transmitted and will cause varying degrees of harm.[35]

To understand the concept of "otherwise qualified" two important definitions are necessary. First, an "otherwise qualified" person is someone who, in spite of his or her handicap, can perform the essential functions of the job. Then, in the event that a handicapped individual is unable to perform the essential functions of the job, were reasonable accommodations made to help the employee? Reasonable accommodations are defined as those that pose neither undue financial nor administrative burdens on an employer.[36]

---

[34] Ibid.

[35] Ibid.

[36] Ibid.

Clearly, the whole issue of AIDS in the work place is very complicated. It seems that much of the burden of dealing with employees who have AIDS will fall on the department of human resources management. It would be inappropriate for human resources managers to attempt to diagnose the condition of the employee; that is a medical function. But once the infection is found and the stage determined, personnel actions within human resources policies will have to be taken. As the disease continues to spread, it may be that additional actions will have to be taken in order for organizations to protect the rights of all their employees, including those suffering from AIDS.

SEXUAL HARASSMENT

Sexual harassment is a form of sex discrimination and as such is a violation of existing federal regulations. It includes behavior such as sexual advances and requests for sexual favors in exchange for promotion, pay increases, and the like. It also includes derogatory or discriminatory remarks regarding one sex or a sexual minority and threats of reprisal following a negative response to sexual overtures.

In 1980 the Equal Employment Opportunity Commission (EEOC) issued guidelines on sexual harassment. The guidelines reflected court decisions stemming from individual lawsuits. In June 1986, the U.S. Supreme Court upheld the EEOC guideline principles in *Meritor Savings Bank v. Vinson* stating that unwelcome sexual advances that create an offensive or hostile working environment violate Title VII of the Civil Rights Act.

Today, employer liability for sexual harassment in the work place is considerable. The *Meritor* decision may spawn a new wave of sexual harassment interest, consciousness, and claims on the part of employers and employees alike. In this case, the Supreme Court held that:[37]

---

[37] Bennett-Alexander, Dawn, "Sexual Harassment in the Office," in *Personnel Administrator*, American Society for Personnel Administration, June 1988, 174-187.

1. A cause of action exists for sexual harassment as a form of sex discrimination where the employee loses or is denied tangible job benefits ("quid pro quo" [this for that] sexual harassment) or is subjected to sexual comments, requests, or activities in the work place that create a hostile, intimidating or offensive atmosphere.
2. The EEOC guidelines can be used to determine what activities are considered as constituting sexual harassment, what an employer can do to lessen or avoid liability, and what an employer may be liable for in sexual harassment claims.
3. Testimony regarding a claimant's provocative dress or discussion of personal fantasies may be considered irrelevant evidence and may be used to show that the sexual requests by the alleged perpetrator were not "unwelcome," as the EEOC guidelines require they must be in order for a claim to be actionable.
4. An employer is not automatically liable for sexual harassment committed by a supervisory employee.
5. When a sexual harassment claim is brought, it is not required that the supervisor who perpetrated the alleged act possess the authority to hire or fire in order to be deemed a supervisor who can bind an employer by his/her actions.
6. An employer's general antidiscrimination policy does not serve as a sexual harassment policy to insulate an employer from liability in sexual harassment cases.
7. If an employee fails to use an employer's complaint procedure to report sexual harassment, it does not automatically exclude the employee from bringing a sexual harassment claim.
8. A sexual harassment claim can be brought by an employee even if the employee consented to the activity. Voluntariness is not a defense an employer can use to avoid liability in a sexual harassment suit.

If employers heed the guidelines the Supreme Court has provided in the *Meritor* case, they improve their chances of avoiding sexual harassment suits and defending against them should they arise. Future court cases on sexual harassment should serve to fine tune the policies, procedures, and approaches already adopted by employers to protect both themselves and their employees in the work place.[38]

It will be some years yet before people at work become accustomed to the highly integrated conditions of the work place. The transition from the "old days" to the new work climate will be facilitated by the policies mentioned above. Additionally, personnel at work will have to be trained in ways of handling job-related interpersonal relations to make them smooth and proper and to avoid incidences of sexual harassment and the creation of environments that are intolerable to protected groups as well as to the rest of the work force.

COMPARABLE WORTH

The issue of comparable worth centers around the view that some persons are paid on a different wage scale in jobs that are different from each other but are of comparable worth to the organization. In general, the cases that have been brought before the courts charge that there is a wage gap among different job categories resulting in gender-based discrimination. The objective in filing these cases is to bring about abandonment of the current market wage determination system and replace it with an administered wage system based on "comparable worth."

The American Society for Personnel Administration, representing the field of human resources management, has been in the forefront of efforts to professionalize the field. Concerning compensation, ASPA has devoted enormous energy toward

[38] Ibid.

increasing the state of the art and the proficiency of compensation managers to develop accurate and fair compensation systems and plans. This approach is intended to ensure that bias does not enter compensation systems found in the work place.

The courts have repeatedly and consistently rejected the comparable worth argument that discrimination is present whenever wage differences that cannot be connected to economic factors exist. The courts have also recognized that an endorsement of the vague concept of "comparable worth" would necessitate massive involvement by the courts in restructuring and governing one of the most sensitive aspects of the economy. Such involvement is inconsistent with the legislative history of the Equal Pay Act and Title VII of the Civil Rights Act. This kind of involvement by the courts would put them in the business of managing corporations, which they are not competent to do.

Human resources management professionals are firmly committed to equal pay for equal work, to the principles of affirmative action, and to continued effort to ensure that all persons are afforded equal opportunity to compete for every job. These are appropriate solutions to the issue of compensation inequalities, which underlie the comparable worth controversy. Properly designed and administered compensation programs afford the greatest opportunity to ensure that bias does not enter into setting pay. These programs also ensure that the adoption of legislation or regulations embracing the concept of comparable worth is unnecessary and inappropriate given our economic system. Companies of all sizes are encouraged to perform regular compensation or job evaluation studies according to established professional standards. The issue of comparable worth will not go away, however, until organizations can demonstrate fair and equitable compensation practices over a prolonged period of time, and the employees of these organizations are convinced of the fairness of the system and the worth of their individual jobs. It is obvious that departments of human resources will be deeply involved in comparable worth issues, working to achieve the conditions just described.

NEW DUTIES FOR HUMAN RESOURCES MANAGEMENT

Since the early years of this century, the number of duties assigned to personnel departments has been increasing. Indicators show this trend continuing. A duty that has been closely related to human resources management is that of payroll. This function used to be established somewhere in the finance area of organizations. That was because the finance department had the machinery and know-how to deal with all kinds of money issues, although it might not have handled currency itself. In practice the personnel office sent orders to payroll concerning classification, pay rates, and other relevant information. Payroll then took the appropriate actions to ensure the proper rates of pay took effect. Modern computer technology now permits the function to be performed under the jurisdiction of the human resources department.

A review of the current issues just discussed reveals the extent to which legislation, court decisions, and the findings of such bodies as the National Labor Relations Board, impact the function of human resources management. This strongly suggests that top human resources professionals will have to acquire a thorough knowledge of these matters in order to perform the duties demanded of them. In order to retain control of the human resources function, human resources managers must keep abreast of legal developments in the field.

OCCUPATIONAL SAFETY AND HEALTH

In modern society, employers are expected to provide working conditions that protect the health and safety of their employees.[39] This requires providing a work environment that safeguards employees from such hazards as atmospheric contami-

---

[39] Sherman, Bohlander, and Chruden, *Managing Human Resources*, 575.

nants, high noise levels, unguarded machinery, and radiation. State laws and administrative procedures have traditionally prescribed the safeguards that must be taken by employers and have provided for inspections in order to determine compliance. In an effort to assist and encourage the states in their attempts to ensure safe and healthful working conditions, Congress enacted the Occupational Safety and Health Act of 1970 (OSHA).

Responsibilities for implementing OSHA are divided between the Department of Labor and the Department of Health and Human Services. The Assistant Secretary of Labor revises, modifies, or revokes existing standards or creates new ones. The National Institute of Safety and Health (NIOSH) in the Department of Health and Human Services is responsible for doing the research. OSHA is an agency of the Department of Labor, and it administers the act.

Safety and health standards and regulations, which are published in the *Federal Register,* cover every conceivable health and safety problem for all employers engaged in business affecting interstate commerce. The act provides for the exclusion of certain groups that are covered by comparable safety and health acts.

The OSHA standards and regulations are published in great detail and fill many volumes. They cover standards for the work place, as well as worker-employee standards for protective clothing, first aid, and administration requirements.

Any employee who believes that a violation of a job safety or health standard exists that threatens physical harm or poses imminent danger may request an inspection. Where an investigation by a Labor Department safety inspector reveals a violation, the employer is issued a written citation describing the specific nature of the violation. The citation, which must be posted at or near each place where a violation occurred, fixes a reasonable time for the abatement of the violation. After issuance of a citation, the employer is notified of the penalty, if any, to be assessed. Willful or repeated violation of the act's requirements by employers may incur monetary penalties of up to $10,000 for each violation.

Employers are required to keep and make available to the federal government records on certain activities and reports on work-related deaths, injuries, and illnesses. Employers may also be required to maintain accurate records of employee exposure to potentially toxic materials or harmful physical agents that are required to be measured or monitored.

Since OSHA holds employers responsible for making their employees wear safety equipment, employers must engage in safety training and be prepared to discipline employees for noncompliance with safety rules. As a result, many grievances have been filed by employees who have refused to work in unsafe conditions and have been subjected to management discipline. It is also reported that some disgruntled union personnel have filed complaints directly with OSHA and then deliberately sabotaged the employer, creating violations only minutes before the inspector arrived. Such incidents are made possible by the fact that OSHA does not provide for employees' responsibility for any safety violations discovered by the OSHA inspector. The burden of compliance rests solely with the employer. However, the employee does have the responsibility of complying with established safety rules, and deliberate refusal to comply becomes grounds for termination under the federal law.

The OSHA requirements for keeping records of work-related injuries and illnesses are desirable because all factors that led or contributed to an accident or illness should be identified and reported on prescribed forms. From such records analyses can be made and corrective action taken where causes may be identified. In some cases accidents result primarily from unsafe equipment. In others, human factors appear to be responsible.

The following items could serve as a checklist of items to be observed periodically for safe conditions.

Fire Protection

Access to fire equipment
Exit lights/doors/signs
Extinguishers charged/properly located

First Aid

First aid kits
Stretchers, fire blankets, oxygen

General Area

Aisle clearance/markings
Floor openings, safeguards
Piping systems
Railings, stairs
Ventilation
Wall damage

Housekeeping

Break area/latrines
Floors
Machines
Rodent, insect, vermin control
Vending machines, food protection
Waste disposal

Illumination – Wiring

Frayed/defective wiring
Hazardous location
Lights on during shutdown
Machinery not grounded
Overloading circuits
Wall outlets

Machinery

Emergency stops not operational
Guards in place
Operating instructions posted
Maintenance performed on machines
Platforms/ladders/catwalks
Unattended machines running

Material Storage

Hazardous substances and flammables not properly stored
Improper lighting
Improper stacking/loading/securing

Tools

Condition of hand tools
Power tool wiring
Safe storage

Vehicles

Failure to obey traffic rules
Operating defective vehicle
Reckless speeding/operation
Unauthorized use

The term *accident-prone* is often used to describe those individuals who have more than their share of accidents. Two theories may explain accident proneness. The first theory states that accidents tend to occur in an unrewarding psychological work environment that is not conducive to a high level of alertness. The richer the climate in economic and psychological opportunities, the higher the level of alertness. This theory proposes that if the work climate provides the freedom to set reasonably attainable goals, the workers feel themselves to be significant participants and that this, in turn, leads to habits of alertness, problem raising, and problem solving. Studies on the effect of psychological climate on accident behavior lend considerable support to this theory.

The second theory holds that unusual, negative, and distracting stress upon the individual increases the tendency to have accidents. Negative stresses include diseases, toxic materials, temperature excesses, poor illumination, excessive noise level, excessive physical work strain, and excessive hours.

An emerging aspect of OSHA is that of occupational alcoholism. Organizations are establishing occupational alcoholism programs that are intended to deal with the worker who has a drinking problem that affects the performance of work. Most of these programs try to deal with the alcoholic through a series of counseling sessions, which the worker attends on a voluntary basis. The organizations usually support the programs financially and find that they are a worthwhile investment because they save the worker for the company, they keep the worker from being fired and thus becoming a burden on the community, and they save the company the cost of hiring and training a new worker. Most programs deal with many types of substance abuse, including drugs and alcohol.

CHAPTER 10

ORGANIZATIONS AND INFORMATION

Professional organizations and many labor unions have a vested interest in the dissemination of information about personnel management. There are a number of organizations that will provide help to those who seek career information about work in the personnel administration and industrial relations field. To obtain this assistance, you should write the organization and request information concerning what helpful data and assistance are available to those seeking careers in personnel and industrial relations. Most organizations have printed pamphlets and brochures that explain their roles and information concerning the services they provide.

Organizations that might interest you include the following:

AFL-CIO
815 16th Street, NW
Washington, D.C. 20006

American Management Association (AMA)
135 West 50th Street
New York, N.Y. 10020

American Society for Personnel Administration (ASPA)
606 N. Washington Street
Alexandria, Va. 22314

American Society for Training and Development (ASTD)
1630 Duke Street
Alexandria, Va. 22313

Bureau of Labor Statistics
U.S. Department of Labor
3rd Street & Constitution Avenue, NW
Washington, D.C. 20210

Bureau of National Affairs (BNA)
1231 25th Street, NW
Washington, D.C. 20037

Equal Employment Opportunity Commission (EEOC)
2401 E Street, NW
Washington, D.C. 20506

Federal Mediation and Conciliation Service
2100 K Street, NW
Washington, D.C. 20427

Internal Revenue Service (IRS)
111 Constitution Avenue, NW
Washington, D.C. 20224

International Personnel Management Association (IPMA)
1313 E. 60th Street
Chicago, Ill. 60637

National Association for the Advancement of Colored People (NAACP)
1790 Broadway
New York, N.Y. 10019

National Association of Manufacturers (NAM)
1776 F Street
Washington, D.C. 20006

Occupational Safety and Health Administration (OSHA)
200 Constitution Ave., NW
Washington, D.C. 20210

Office of Federal Contract Compliance (OFCC)
200 Constitution Ave., NW
Washington, D.C. 20210

Pension Benefit Guaranty Corporation
P.O. Box 7119
Washington, D.C. 20044

Don't overlook the possibility of obtaining career information from local organizations and agencies such as the Chamber of Commerce and the state unemployment agency. Additionally, information and assistance may be available from the local offices of various individual labor unions. Some of those that have been active in this regard, in addition to the AFL-CIO, are the Teamsters (IBT) and the Machinists (IAM).

The brochure from the American Society for Personnel Administration is entitled, "Careers in Human Resources Management," and includes information on the following topics:

Personnel function
Personnel office
Personnel specialists
- Employment and placement
- Training
- Labor relations
- Wage and salary administration
- Benefits and services
- Preparation

Personal requirements
Salaries
Outlook for the future

There is also the possibility of finding information through student organizations. Many colleges and universities have student chapters of the American Society for Personnel Administration.

ADDITIONAL SOURCES OF INFORMATION

1. "Careers in Human Resources Management," American Society for Personnel Administration, 606 North

Washington Street, Alexandria, Va. 22314. Six pages. Ask for current revision as well as other available pamphlets and booklets relating to careers in personnel and labor relations.

2. "Personnel Workers," a section of the *Occupational Outlook Handbook*, issued biannually by the U.S. Department of Labor, Bureau of Labor Statistics.
3. "Hospital Personnel Director," American Hospital Association, 840 North Lake Shore Drive, Chicago, Ill. 60611. Four pages, free.
4. Information about personnel careers in government may be obtained through free pamphlets available from the International Personnel Management Association, 1313 East 60th Street, Chicago, Ill. 60637.
5. "Personnel, a Challenging Career in Management," International Association of Personnel Women, 358 Fifth Avenue, New York, N.Y. 10001. Single copy, free.
6. "The Human Equation—Working in Personnel for the Federal Government," U.S. Office of Personnel Management, Washington, D.C. 20415. Free.
7. "Occupational Briefs," Chronicle Guidance Publishing Company, Inc., Moravia, N.Y. 13118.
8. "SRA Occupational Briefs," Science Research Associates, Inc., 155 North Wacker Drive, Chicago, Ill. 60606.
9. "Career Information: A Directory of Free Materials for Counselors and Teachers," Sextant Systems, Inc., Western Station, Box 4283, Milwaukee, Wis. 53210.
10. "A Career in Business Administration," a filmstrip from Pathescope Educational Films, Inc., The Associated Press, 71 Weyman Avenue, New Rochelle, N.Y. 10802.
11. *The Occupational Thesaurus*, Lehigh University, Bethlehem, Pa.
12. *The Dictionary of Occupational Titles*. See your local school library.
13. Don't forget the following additional sources of information:

a. The high school career counseling office
b. The high school college counseling office
c. State employment security agencies
d. Private employment agencies
e. Newspaper advertising
f. National Career Information Center, local office
g. U.S. Office of Personnel Management
h. Local offices of AFL-CIO unions
i. Local offices of independent unions
j. Local chapters of professional societies

BIBLIOGRAPHY

Bennett-Alexander, Dawn. "Sexual Harassment in the Office." *Personnel Administrator.* American Society for Personnel Administration, June 1988.

Bolles, Richard Nelson. *What Color Is Your Parachute?* Berkeley: Ten Speed Press, 1988.

Burack, Elmer H. and Nicholas J. Mathys. *Career Management in Organizations.* Lake Forest, Ill.: Brace-Park Press, 1980.

College Cost Book: College Board Annual Survey of Colleges, 1988. New York: College Entrance Examination Board.

Davis, Keith. *Human Behavior at Work.* 5th ed. New York: McGraw-Hill Book Company, 1977.

Faze, James. "Parental leave measure reintroduced in Senate." *Resource.* Alexandria, Va.: American Society for Personnel Management, July 1988.

Franklin, Geralyn McClure and Robert K. Robinson. "AIDS and the Law." *Personnel Administrator.* American Society for Personnel Administration, April 1988.

Glueck, William F. *Personnel: A Diagnostic Approach.* 3rd ed. Plano, Tex.: Business Publications, Inc., 1982.

Ling, Cyril Curtis. *The Management of Personnel Relations.* Homewood, Ill.: Richard D. Irwin, Inc., 1965.

Mathis, Robert L. and John H. Jackson. *Personnel/Human Resource Management.* 5th ed. St. Paul, Minn.: West Publishing Company, 1988.

McGregor, Douglas. *The Human Side of Enterprise*. New York: McGraw-Hill Book Company, Inc., 1960.

Place, Irene. *Opportunities in Business Management*. Lincolnwood, Ill.: National Textbook Company, 1986.

Ropp, Kirland. "HR Management for All It's Worth." *Personnel Administrator*. ASPA/Hansen 1987 Human Resource Management Compensation Survey. American Society for Personnel Administration.

Sherman, Arthur W., Jr., George W. Bohlander and Herbert J. Chruden. *Managing Human Resources*. 8th ed. Cincinnati: South-Western Publishing Co., 1988.

Steade, Richard D. and James R. Lowry. *Business: An Introduction*. 11th ed. Cincinnati: South-Western Publishing Co., 1987.

U.S. Department of Labor. Bureau of Labor Statistics. *National Survey of Professional, Administrative, Technical, and Clerical Pay: Private Service Industries*. Bulletin 2290. Washington: Government Printing Office, 1987.

U.S. Department of Labor. Bureau of Labor Statistics. *Occupational Outlook Handbook, 1988-89*. Bulletin 2300. Washington: Government Printing Office, 1988.

The World Almanac and Book of Facts. New York: Newspaper Enterprise Association, Inc., 1988.

Yoder, Dale and Herbert G. Heneman, Jr., eds. *ASPA Handbook of Personnel and Industrial Relations*. Washington: The Bureau of National Affairs, Inc., 1979.

Yoder, Dale and Paul D. Staudohar. *Personnel Management and Industrial Relations*. 7th ed. Englewood Cliffs, N.J.: Prentice-Hall, Inc., 1982.